Big things com
sage packed in
use of scripture and personal experiences, Joyce shows her
readers that Satan is the Father of Lies and God is the Great
Truth Teller. Joyce's ability to use her own life experiences to
reveal God's truth to others is amazing! Her honesty, transparency and humility are both rare and refreshing. Because
of this, she is incredibly sensitive to the Spirit of God working in and around her. Thank you, Joyce for being a willing
servant devoted to sharing His truth with a hurting world!

—LaDonna Alexander
Biblical Counselor –Little River, SC

In her newest book, *Sticks and Stones*, Joyce Schneider
opens up her heart and shares her life in hopes that others
will see the goodness of God and let him heal their past.
We all have issues and sin that we think we've dealt with,
but oftentimes we put a bandage on the problem, thinking
we cured it, but in reality it is festering beneath the surface,
causing doubt, discouragement, and hopelessness. Joyce
takes the reader on a journey through the experiences of
their life and shows them how with God and his people,
you can overcome. This book is a must for those who are
hurting and struggling, and it is a great reminder of God's
power in the realm of forgiveness and victorious living.

—Sherrinda Ketchersid
Writer – Ft. Worth, TX

This book is, as Joyce Schneider states, "A message of healing and hope for others who are hurting." As Joyce shares
the deep wounds of her heart and how healing has taken
place, she gives Christ's path of hope and healing to other

wounded hearts. As she says, "When I finally allowed God to rule over my life, my life started to really change." Those reading the comfort and hope offered by Joyce will also find their lives changed.

—Lynn H. Mosher
Writer - Louisville, KY

When I Look at Joyce Schneider and see the total transformation that I have been privileged to observe, all I can say is "Glory to God." She has renewed her mind through her love of God's Word and allowed Him to impact every part of who she is and what she does. The power of *words* entrapped her, but the power of *God's Word* has freed her to a life of abundance. This book is a transformational journey to freedom, not just for Joyce, but for anyone who is believing the lies. As you read this story, allow God to shine his light of truth into your darkest places and you too will be changed. "...Looking to Jesus the author and finisher of our faith." Enjoy the journey.

—Andrew DeLong
Senior Pastor, Tree of Life Church – Naples, FL

STICKS
~and~ **STONES**
May Break My Bones

But Words Can Kill My Spirit

STICKS
~and~ STONES
May Break My Bones

But Words Can Kill My Spirit

Joyce Schneider

Cover design by Kellie Southerland
Interior design by Leah LeFlore

Published in the United States of America

ISBN: 978-1545084366
1. Religion, Christian Life, Personal Growth
2. Religion, Christian Life, Spiritual Growth
17.03.31

Dedication

This book is dedicated to all the hurting souls who are believing the lies. May you find God's truth within you.

Acknowledgments

It never ceases to amaze me when I reach the point in my writing where I get to give thanks to those who have helped me make this book a reality. As I have said before, it does take a village to create a book, and I wish to give thanks to my own special village for assisting me in bringing *Sticks and Stones...* into fruition.

It is such an honor to be able to share the stories of my life with you, sharing what God has been teaching me through the journey. I pray the lessons in these pages will bless and encourage you as much as they have blessed and encouraged me.

To Cindy Hollingsworth, my very special friend and mentor, I can only say you are truly the best! You are always so willing to help me in any way you can, and you are always there to support and encourage me to take that next step. I love you, my friend. Thank you for always speaking truth to me.

To all my Bible girls and online friends who continually encourage, support, and pray me through this journey, I so appreciate you!

To my friend, Janet Brink, who one day said to me, "If you're not sure, Joyce...," and introduced me to Jesus, the love of my life.

To my very special friend and business partner, Vicki

Gardner, you never stop supporting and encouraging me. Thank you for believing in me. You are so very dear to my heart.

To my parents, Carolyn and Gerald Prouty, thank you for your love and support and your constant encouragement.

To my two little men, Carson and Chase, I love you both so very much. You are my heroes, and I thank you for teaching Mommy so many wonderful lessons. I want to be just like you when I grow up!

As for my Bobby—God surely knew what He was doing when He brought you into my life. You are a constant source of strength and encouragement to me. You are truly one of a kind! Thank you for allowing me to share our life with the world. It takes a very special man to do that, and you are most certainly special! I love you forever!

Last, but certainly not least—I always save the best for last! Thank you, Lord Jesus! Thank you for giving me these lessons to allow me to grow closer to you and to encourage others! It's been such an exciting journey, and I can hardly wait to see what tomorrow brings! Thank you for allowing me to share your love with others, but most of all, Lord Jesus, I thank you for giving me a life that is full to overflowing! I truly could never have imagined life could be so abundant. You are my friend, my Savior, my Lord, and my life! I love you with all my heart and with all my soul! Thank You! Thank You! Thank You!

Table of Contents

The Girl

Something was terribly wrong with the girl. She couldn't put her finger on it, but she just felt so empty inside. Each day was becoming a little harder to get through than the day before. On the surface, life should have been grand. The boy was working at a job he loved. He was home at night and on the weekends. The little boys were as cute as buttons. Perfect little angels…blond hair, blue eyes. They were any mother's dream. Yet…the emptiness just wouldn't leave.

One night the pretty lady asked the girl if she was okay. The girl quickly confirmed, yes, she was fine. The lady looked in her eyes and asked again if she was sure. And once again the girl said yes … but as she drove away that night, she wondered why she was so empty inside, she didn't *feel* fine.

The girl got up the courage the next day to email the pretty lady and tell her she wasn't fine, she was struggling. And she didn't know why. The pretty lady said, "Why don't we meet for prayer?" That was the last thing the girl wanted—to go and talk about or pray about her hurts, but she knew that her little family would not survive if she didn't fix her heart.

So she met with the pretty lady and Jesus came into her heart and healed the hurts that had been festering inside for so very long. The girl couldn't believe the freedom that came into her life that night; the chains were broken, the weights lifted.

And she's never been the same since.

The Stuff That Gets Stuck Inside

I was talking to my sister on the phone one day and she was telling me about an acquaintance of hers who jumped from the Skyway Bridge in St. Petersburg that afternoon.

Then she asked me, "What would cause someone to do such a thing?"

I did have an answer for her, in fact, it was just one word.

Hopelessness…

When a woman loses her hope, well, she loses her desire for life. And this poor woman took that one step farther and actually ended her own life.

As I talked with my sister, trying to comfort her, my thoughts kept returning to my own days of hopelessness.

How many times had I considered taking my own life?

Sometimes it was simply a fleeting thought. Other times a plan was actually conceived, but, for whatever reason, never found completion, thank the Lord.

Drawing from my own experience, the one word that was at the root of such discouragement and depression is *hopelessness.*

Despondent is a synonym of *hopelessness* and this description pretty much says it all:

"Despondent always suggests melancholy and depression; it refers to an emotional state rather than to an intellectual judgment", Webster's Dictionary tells us.

It is an emotional reaction, not an intelligent assessment. So the question arises again, how does a person get so emotionally overwhelmed that she is willing to give up everything, including her own life?

I actually have an idea as to how that can happen.

We get lies or false beliefs stuck inside of us that can distort our vision. We don't see life as it really is, rather we see the world through a veil of deception, and this causes serious problems in all areas of our lives. And the saddest part of this is *we don't even know we are being deceived.*

My hope in writing this book is to help others realize that it's natural to have lies stuck inside us; the world is a very cruel place. It loves nothing better than to beat us up, but it's very important to understand this concept and get to the root of the deception, the sooner the better.

I like to use this illustration in explaining this concept.

Imagine that you were shot with a BB gun when you were a small child, and the BB was lodged in your calf. For whatever reason, you chose to leave that BB in your body. Maybe you were afraid if you told your mother you were playing with a BB gun, the consequences of that would outweigh leaving the BB inside of you, in your mind.

After some time had passed, the wound entrance would heal and no one would really know that you carried a BB around in your leg. But your body would know it; your leg would not function properly, and before long that BB would fester inside of you. Eventually it would cause serious damage to your leg and possibly the rest of your body.

That BB must come out for you to be whole. It will be painful removing the BB, and you will have an open wound for a time, but one day the leg will be completely healed if the BB is removed.

The same holds true of the lies that get stuck inside us. The lie might be something as innocent as your brother calling you *fat* when you were a child, something that is quite common in sibling relationships. But that lie, that you are fat, might find a home inside you and create a lifelong issue of eating disorders for you.

Or maybe you were molested as a teenager, and the shame and guilt of that travesty follows you throughout your life, destroying any chance of a true, meaningful relationship.

There are so many scenarios that illustrate this point, I could not begin to list them all, but what I can say is this: each one of us has struggled with bad habits, hurts, and hang-ups, and these negative behaviors and emotional states are often the result of some falsehood that we've allowed to control our emotions and thoughts, which then interfered with our healthy mental and spiritual development.

I believe that once we remove the original root lie or issue, we can begin the healing process to become whole—emotionally, spiritually, and even physically. Because our physical body houses our emotions, it would only be natural that once our emotions are based on what is true and are no longer a destructive force, our physical bodies would have the opportunity to be healed as well.

This book isn't filled with scientific jargon. I've never been able to read that stuff, so I most certainly can't write it. But what it *is* filled with is personal experience—why I believe what I believe and the positive results that I've experienced in my own life by rooting out the lies and letting Jesus heal my hurts once and for all.

This journey towards healing all started one evening by a simple statement on my part, followed by a personal observation.

"I'm fine."…

But…if I'm fine, why do I feel so empty inside?

Have you ever voiced those thoughts? Do you wonder what is wrong with you? You know you're not right inside, but you have no clue what is wrong.

I spent so much of my life saying, "I'm fine," that I actually began to believe it. And why not? My mind was filled with one lie after another to the point that I could not even begin to decipher the truth.

And the really crazy part of it all is I am a normal, (well somewhat normal) wife, mother, friend, Christian.

I am the girl next door, the soccer mom, the Sunday school teacher. I am just like you (maybe a little shorter).

It all started when I realized that I was living a lie. I wasn't fine, but I had no idea why I was so miserable inside.

I knew the Lord, and I was on fire to learn all I could about him, but it seemed like regardless of the head knowledge I was acquiring, I remained tormented inside and felt as though I was living in a vacuum.

One day Bobby finally asked me,

"Joyce, how long are you going to be like this?"

I didn't have to ask him what he was talking about. I simply shrugged and answered, "I don't know."

I was living in a state of anguish. I didn't know why, but I needed to know. I wasn't being a good mother to my boys, a good wife to my husband or a good follower of Jesus.

I began to seriously ponder my life, and I finally realized

part of what was going on. I was still suffering terrible grief over two prior miscarriages, and I had unrelenting shame and guilt built up inside that had been festering for almost twenty years over things in my past.

I had lived a very wild life before I was married. I was drinking and doing drugs at age fifteen. When I went away to college, I started sleeping with guys. I found myself pregnant and alone at age twenty-five. I really didn't know what to do; I just knew I needed to be 'un-pregnant', so I ended up in an abortion clinic one morning, ending my baby's life. I knew in my head that was the wrong thing to do, but I wasn't thinking clearly. Drugs, alcohol, and a constant stream of men in my life had really taken their toll on my emotional and mental state. I made many wrong decisions during this season of my life, but the abortion seemed to be the one thing that I could never forgive myself for.

It constantly ate at my spirit and my mind, although I would never discuss it with anyone. It was my secret sin that ate away a bit more of my soul each and every day.

I realized I needed help and that I wasn't going to be able to pretend this away, and I confessed to a good friend that I was still suffering extreme grief from my past miscarriages, although at that point, I still wasn't ready to share my abortion story with her.

My friend suggested we meet for prayer, and we simply asked God to reveal to me what was holding me back from having true peace and joy in my life.

What was the band-aid on my emotions covering up?

The last thing I really wanted to do was sit down with someone and spill my guts, but I was desperate for help, and when we are desperate, we do uncomfortable things. But because I stepped out of my comfort zone, I was able to experience God's healing power in my life, true healing not the pretend 'I'm fine' variety that I was so used to portraying.

You see, I had confessed my sins to Jesus when I accepted him as my Savior, and I knew he forgave me. But I was so filled with guilt and shame over my past that I had never forgiven *myself;* I had never allowed God's forgiveness to penetrate my heart, never allowed the healing process to begin.

But that night during prayer time, the disgusting band-aid of self-condemnation that I had let cover me for so long was finally ripped off. I felt as if a great weight was lifted from me! Chains were broken. I was set free!

I went home that night, opened my Bible and came upon a verse that says, "Come near to God and He will come near to you." (James 4:8)

I knew that was true; as I came nearer, God would be there for me.

This was the beginning of my quest for truth within. It's been an interesting journey, though admittedly, a painful one. It hurts to dig out those BBs, and just when I thought they were all out, another one would begin to surface.

But what I've learned through the process is this: We must root out the lies; we must let Jesus heal our hurts, if we are to live happy, healthy lives for him.

Jesus did not die on that cross for us to limp through this life, to be defeated and discouraged and hopeless, to throw ourselves off bridges or overdose on drugs or hide behind the façade of "I'm fine." No, he came so that we might have life and live it to abundance. His Word tells us:

"The thief comes only to steal and kill and destroy; I

have come that they may have life, and have it to the full." (John 10:10)

My prayer for you is that as you read through this story, you will examine your own life and start asking the Holy Spirit to reveal the root of your issues, to show you if there are lies distorting your vision or BBs stuck inside you, hindering your healing.

And once those lies are revealed, I pray the Holy Spirit helps you to understand how to replace them with God's truth so that you can live a healthy, whole, productive life for him.

Some of these stories are painful to share. But I've found through my journey that if I share my experiences, I always find others going through similar challenges. And when these people hear that someone else is as messed up or more messed up than they are, well, somehow that just helps.

It helps us to see how the enemy can use innocent statements to distort our thinking and play with our emotions. And how, by placing truth in front of those lies, they immediately vanish.

Someone once asked me how these results could happen so quickly. I know it sounds too good to be true, but think about this scenario:

Suppose you are taking a walk and up ahead you see a snake on the path. Your heart would probably start beating rather quickly. I know I would be shaking. But as you get closer, you realize that the snake is really just a branch that blew off a nearby tree; it cannot harm you. Immediately, the fear of the snake vanishes. Your belief that a snake was lying in your path was based on faulty understanding, and when the truth is revealed, the fear is immediately dispelled.

The same concept applies to the lies inside us—when they are replaced with truth, the veil of deception is lifted, the BBs are removed, and healing can begin.

Yes…there *is* hope for us. And his name is Jesus!

The happiness which brings enduring worth to life is not the superficial happiness that is dependent on circumstances. It is the happiness and contentment that fills the soul even in the midst of the most distressing circumstances and the most bitter environment. It is the kind of happiness that grins when things go wrong and smiles through the tears. The happiness for which our souls ache is one undisturbed by success or failure, one which will root deeply inside us and give inward relaxation, peace, and contentment, no matter what the surface problems may be. That kind of happiness stands in need of no outward stimulus.

—Billy Graham[1]

I'm Fine

I was watching TV the other night and I saw two different women say, "I'm fine," when in truth, their lives were spinning out of control. Last week, I shared my story with a group of women. I explained to them how I used to cover up my pain and guilt in front of others by always saying, "I'm fine." Eventually I started asking myself the question, *If I were fine, why did I feel so empty inside?* That query led me to answers and those answers led me to Jesus who healed my heart from the inside out.

One of my friends gave me a card at the end of our evening together. On it was written these words:

Freaked out
Insecure
Neurotic
Emotional

That was a pretty good description of my mental state when I'd say I was *fine*. I was either freaked out or insecure or neurotic or emotional or all four rolled into one!

I don't usually say "I'm fine" any longer. I say, "I'm good." And that, my friend, is a nice place to be. When I say this, I'm not saying I don't have problems, and I'm surely not saying my life is perfect. On the contrary, some days it seems like all I have are problems. Face it; life can be a real challenge at times. But I can honestly say that even in the midst of the struggles, I have a peace which can only come from God, and that is good.

I don't have to try to smile and put on my fake face and pretend like everything is fine. Through the love of Jesus, I have discovered how to have peace, even in the midst of the craziness of life.

So, the next time you catch yourself saying, "I'm fine," I would encourage you to stop and ask yourself, *Am I really?*

———————————

Father, thank you for changing my heart. Thank you for taking the hurt and replacing it with your most amazing love! I know that so many people are hurting inside. I pray that they will allow you to come into their lives and take away their pain. Bring them your peace in the midst of their storms.

> I Love You Jesus.
> In Your Name I Pray,
> Amen

God's promise for today:

"The fruit of righteousness will be peace; the effect of righteousness will be quietness and confidence forever."
Isaiah 32:17

"Do not be anxious about anything, but in everything, by prayer and petition, with thanksgiving, present

your requests to God. And the peace of God, which
transcends all understanding, will guard your
hearts and your minds in Christ Jesus."
Philippians 4:6, 7

"But the fruit of the Spirit is love, joy, peace, patience,
kindness, goodness, faithfulness, gentleness and self-control."
Galatians 5:22, 23

"Those who hope in the Lord will renew their strength.
They will soar on wings like eagles; they will run and
not grow weary; they will walk and not be faint."
Isaiah 40:31

Lies of the Past— Victory over the Darkness

One Sunday afternoon, my friend, Cindy, asked me to share a short testimony for the new class that she was teaching from the book *Victory over the Darkness* by Neil Anderson. I knew that there would be a lot of hurting people in the class, and I was trying to think what part of my story to share with them so that they could see my personal victory over my own darkness.

As I pondered my past, some very unsettling memories came up. One in particular was quite disturbing.

I had never blocked out the incident, but I can't say how long it had been since I'd thought of it. I know it had been a very long time.

Many years ago, when I was in my twenties, I woke up one morning in a strange house, with people that I didn't know. This was not really that unusual in those days. I was always going to one late night party or another, and ended up crashing wherever I fell, literally, most nights. But something was different about this morning,

I realized that I'd had sex the previous night and even worse that it had not been *conventional* sex, but rather, I'd been sodomized. Now, I really had no memory of the incident, but it became apparent when I woke up. In essence, I had been raped.

I got up, gathered my clothes, and found my way to a

friend's house, where I curled up in a ball on her couch, not sharing what happened to me with anyone. I know I stayed there one day, it might have been longer. I finally pulled myself back together and went on with my life, but this incident messed with my head.

This is what popped into my head on that Sunday afternoon when I was pondering what to share. Not the trauma of experiencing it, as I had no memory of the actual event, but the emotions that came with the realization of what had happened afterwards: anger, humiliation, shame, guilt, and rejection.

I had been used and in a very unpleasant manner.

I kept trying to dismiss these thoughts from my head but to no avail. That night I tried to sleep, but I tossed and turned all night long, unpleasant memories flooding my thoughts. I got up the next morning with a heavy heart, realizing that I needed to go to Jesus with this concern.

After I got the boys to school, I ended up in my office under my prayer quillow; a small quilt-like blanket that my Grandmother made for me. I was determined to allow God to show me yet one more root or lie that needed to be removed. I had been sharing with Cindy a bit about my situation, and during the conversation, I admitted to her that I felt like I was to blame for this happening to me, as I kept putting myself in vulnerable situations.

She assured me that although, yes, I had put myself in a vulnerable spot, what happened to me was *not* my fault, I had been a victim of someone else's perversion, and I was *not responsible for their misdeeds.*

It was apparent to me that God wanted me to release this incident to him, so down onto my knees I knelt.

As I prayed for God to reveal his truth, I immediately

sensed a heavy darkness around me. Then in my mind, I saw a picture of a chicken running around, without its head.

Odd. I continued praying and I was reminded of another similar incident that had occurred to me before I moved to Florida. That time, I had been aware of what was happening, and was able to stop the man from violating me. Then it was brought back to my memory, my very first experience with sex and the feelings and emotions I experienced that night. The movie in my mind continued playing and it seemed to be rolling through all the men in my life who had hurt me physically and emotionally. It was quite intense, and I experienced a huge release of emotion. *Why had they hurt me?* was the question that was rumbling through my mind.

After this, it seemed like God showed me that the enemy had crept into my life, in the form of drugs and alcohol, and he'd stolen my mind. I was the chicken with my head cut off, making no sense of anything, running aimlessly through life, getting myself into one bad situation after another.

All of these harmful situations occurred when I was drinking and using drugs. Now, hear me here, I am not making excuses, I made these wrong choices, but throughout them, I wasn't in my right mind. My mind was gone.

I never did any of this crazy stuff when I was sober. I was a pretty *regular* person. But once I started drinking or taking drugs, it seems like I just went wild! No holds barred!

As I sat and pondered this theory, it seemed to me that God was giving me back my mind putting the head back on the chicken, so to speak.

At that point, a chalkboard appeared in my mind, on it were the names of all the men that had hurt me, but as I watched, an eraser appeared, wiping away each and every name, and with each stroke, it erased the hurt and rejection that these men had left in my heart.

It was the wildest thing, watching that eraser just wipe away the pain.

I've learned from past experience that when we remove something negative from inside of us, we need to replace it with something positive or the bad comes back, usually worse than before. I didn't want any more of this junk inside of me, I asked the Lord to fill me up with his love. Immediately, this wonderful, comforting twirling red mass began swirling through my mind. It seemed to be flowing through every part of me with its comfort. It's a bit difficult to put into words; it's one of those things where you had to be there. It was just so sweet to be in the midst of the presence of God.

It was like God was proclaiming all he was to me, while this mass was swirling inside of me. It seemed to be saying, *I will never hurt you. I will never reject you. I will never leave you.*

It was so comforting. He was with me, comforting me, showing me how much he loved me.

I usually get a scripture when I go through this progression; a confirmation of God's promise to me, and today was no different. I kept hearing inside my heart, *I will never leave you nor forsake you.* It was almost like he was letting me know; *I will never hurt you nor reject you.*

I realized that I didn't feel like I was to blame for all the bad that had happened to me, and I didn't feel bad about myself anymore. I felt like I truly was God's precious child.

I want to clarify something. You may not understand *why* it's so important for me to *feel* peace inside, I should live by what I *know*; God loves me and I am forgiven, regardless of how I *feel*.

I will try to explain.

I spent so much of my life being numb, from drugs and alcohol, not thinking of my feelings, not feeling period. Every time I tried to feel, I'd end up hurt and confused. So I decided that being numb was the answer.

But that's not the answer. It's a cop out. When I found Jesus, I started feeling again. However, a lot of the things that I felt didn't feel so great. A lot of bad emotions began to surface.

I loved Jesus, but I still had the yuckiness of my past messing up my emotions. When I learned to face them head on, get to the root and let Jesus help me find the truth in the midst of all the junk, well, at that point was when *real peace* came into my life.

And the peace of God is better than any drug on the market. It's the real deal. And so my goal became to root out *all* the lies, *all* the deception, *all* the bad stuff that I'd bottled up for all those years—to get clean and clear inside so that I truly could live the life that Jesus so desperately wants for all of us.

This is my desire for you as well. So many times we are ashamed of something in our past and we decide the best way to deal with it is to not – to ignore it. But the wounds will not stop hurting until you let Jesus heal them, from the inside out. He so desperately wants to do this for you.

"He heals the brokenhearted and binds up their wounds." Psalm 147:3

So wait before the Lord. Wait in the stillness. And in

that stillness, assurance will come to you. You will know that you are heard; you will know that your Lord ponders the voice of your humble desires; you will hear quiet words spoken to you yourself, perhaps to your grateful surprise and refreshment.

—Amy Carmichael[2]

The Voice of Truth

"Jesus answered, 'I am the way and the truth and the life. No one comes to the Father except through me.'"
John 14:6

One summer day, I didn't have to work and the boys didn't have school. We were hanging out and running errands, not necessarily the boys' favorite pastime. They don't like to ride around with me in my truck. The AC was broken, and they always end up feeling sick after just a few minutes; they just can't handle the heat that goes along with riding around with no AC in Naples in the summer-time.

The boys, especially Carson, tend to fuss at each other when they don't feel well. When Carson is miserable, he wants everyone else to be miserable. As we were driving around, he was fussing at his brother and calling him names. At one point, he began calling him "fat." Now, Chase is far from fat. Chase is eight years old and weighs maybe 40 pounds soaking wet. But Carson likes to call him fat for some reason, and it just annoys Chase to no end.

I listened to their bickering for a bit, then I said, "Chase, are you fat?" His response was, "No". "Then don't listen to your brother," was my reply. And Chase didn't. He ignored Carson and soon Carson stopped teasing him, and then I saw a dog crossing the road, and we started talking about how we hoped the dog wouldn't get hit by a car. The conversation changed and everyone was happy.

Later that day, I was listening to the song "The Voice of Truth" by Casting Crowns; it's about facing the giants in our lives that constantly taunt us, about stepping out of the boat, into the crashing waves that want to swallow us up. The chorus goes like this:

> But the Voice of Truth tells me a different story
> The Voice of Truth says, "Do not be afraid!"
> And the Voice of Truth says, "This is for my glory"
> Out of all the voices calling out to me
> I will choose to listen and believe the Voice of Truth

I used to believe the lies—the lies that I didn't deserve a family, that I deserved all the bad things that had happened to me because I always put myself in vulnerable situations. I believed that I deserved the shame and guilt that was so heavy on my heart, that it was my lot in life. I believed my past made me useless for God's future.

The song ends like this:

> But the stone was just the right size
> To put the giant on the ground
> And the waves they don't seem so high
> On top of them lookin' down
> I soar with the wings of eagles
> When I stop and listen to the sound of Jesus
> Singing over me

One day, I heard a new voice. And it started telling me something different. And as I listened to that voice, my life changed. Day by day, victory by victory, strength by strength; the voice of truth became the voice I chose to listen to and the voice I chose to believe.

I want to encourage you today to stop and listen to the voices you are hearing—let the voice of truth ring forth!

———————————

Father, your Word tells us that you are the way, the truth and the light. Thank you, Lord, for showing me the way through your truth and for lighting my path so that I no longer stumble through the darkness.

I Love You Jesus.
In Your Name I Pray,
Amen

God's promise for today:

"Into your hands I commit my spirit; redeem me, O LORD, the God of truth."
Psalm 31:5

"The Word became flesh and made his dwelling among us. We have seen his glory, the glory of the One and Only, who came from the Father, full of grace and truth."
John 1:14

"Then you will know the truth, and the truth will set you free."
John 8:32

"It is for freedom that Christ has set us free, stand firm, then, and do not let yourselves be burdened again by a yoke of slavery."
Galatians 5:1

Innocent Statements— You Were Supposed To Be a Boy

Sometimes the lies that get stuck inside of us come from words we hear from others. They may be the most innocent of statements. The person saying them has no idea that the enemy will twist them around in our minds and use them to attempt to destroy our spirits.

It is vital that we understand that the person who made the statement is innocent of any wrongdoing. Okay, well maybe your big brother teasing you and calling you "gorilla girl" all your life isn't totally innocent. He should not have teased you and called you names. But the point I want to get across is they are not the ones that turn the statements into lies in your soul.

We have an enemy and he is out to destroy you, and he will use everything possible to do that.

> *"For our struggle is not against flesh and blood, but against the rulers, against the authorities, against the powers of this dark world and against the spiritual forces of evil in the heavenly realms."*
> *Ephesians 6:12*

I've learned that even the most innocent of statements can be the start of a lifetime of self deception.

My friends are always teasing me about how many more layers are going to come off and how many old issues are still deep down inside of me, just waiting for something to stir them up to the top.

I don't really know how many layers are yet to come, but God showed me this was a serious one that needed his attention.

Before I get into this, I want to say a couple of things. I am sharing this because Jesus encouraged me to share it, to get closure. Originally, I never dreamed I would actually put it into a book. It is not something I am comfortable sharing. But sometimes we have to stretch out of our comfort zone. I believe there are many people out there who will benefit from this story. And that is the purpose of this message—to make a difference in other's lives, to help others find healing through Jesus.

There is no hidden agenda to this story; it's simply what happened to me.

One day I was at a friend's hair salon, when one of my guy friends made a statement about me looking butch. He was just teasing me, something about a haircut from my past, but his statement stirred up a trigger in me that just wouldn't go away.

When I was young, I was a real tomboy. I would do boy things, wear boy clothes, and play with boys. My dad called me his *first son* and I spent my early years on tractors and in barns and doing all sorts of *boy* stuff. I never really thought about why I didn't like girl stuff. It was just the way I was.

As I got older, sometimes I would feel like I was not supposed to be a girl that I was really supposed to be a boy. But that made no sense to me. I liked boys; there was always a boy that I had a crush on. It was an odd contradiction one that I didn't understand. So, I simply attributed the questions away in my mind as just growing up stuff, figuring out life, who you are, etc.

Later on in my life, I actually thought about being gay. Now, truly, I don't know if that is something you just one day decide to become. I was just tired of men; how they treated me, how much they hurt me, and I figured I would just find another girl like me who was tired of men, and that would be that. I didn't want a sexual relationship; it was the emotional connection that I was seeking. I just wanted to be with someone who was like me, who wouldn't hurt me.

After the fiasco with my abortion, I had been involved in way too many unhealthy relationships; some for a day, some for a week, one had even went as far as an engagement. But that didn't work out; I found out he'd been cheating on me, and he beat me up one night when I tried to confront him on it. Not so great. And then came the rape incident I shared with you earlier. Honestly, I was just done with men. I figured women might be a safer route.

But that never happened. I guess I really didn't believe in my mind that it was the right thing to do, and then I met a sweet twenty-three year old boy, and we hung out together for about a year, and he was safe and young and innocent and never dreamed of doing anything to hurt me, and the idea of being gay became a distant memory.

But on occasion, out of the blue, those thoughts would pop back up, at the weirdest times, making no sense at all to me. I knew I wasn't gay, I knew I liked men, but sometimes I'd just desire that close bond with another woman— something *safe*, not a sexual thing, just wanting a relationship with someone that I could trust. Men were not trust-worthy in my world. And in my mind, the only sort of love relationship I knew was sexual, and I was hugely confused.

Then I met Bobby, and we ended up getting married a few years later and all those thoughts and confusion disap-peared. And that was pretty much that, or so I thought.

As I mentioned earlier, the incident at the hair salon triggered something inside of me, and these old thoughts started invading my mind. One night, I was doing dishes and I started thinking about my dad and how he used to call me his first son and brag on how well I did the farm work with him, and immediately I had the thought, "You were supposed to be a boy."

I remembered thinking about someone saying to me, at some point in my life that I was supposed to be a boy when I was born. My parents had wanted a boy. They had a little girl, and they were looking for me to be a little boy. I believe this statement was said to me on occasion and somehow in my mind, it started confusion.

I've pondered it on and off my entire life, not really understanding why. And then came the day when my friend made the statement to me about being butch, and it all flew back into my head and I could not get it out.

And so I did what I do when these things start stirring up inside of me, when I start feeling unsettled; I prayed about it. Jesus revealed to me that it was a false belief; he showed me that I am just who I am supposed to be.

Jeremiah 1:5 says, "Before I formed you in the womb I knew you, before you were born I set you apart; I appointed you as a prophet to the nations."

God knew me before I was me, he made me. And he made me a woman. And that is good.

I know this chapter is a bit out of the norm, and I'm sorry. I can assure you it wasn't easy living it. Can you image the confusion that distorted my thoughts for all those years as I was growing up, trying to sort it all out? Especially since I never shared this with anyone. I kept it swirling around in my head all those years, embarrassed to share it with anyone.

Not a lot of fun, I can assure you.

So, after this revelation, I called my friend, and shared my story with her.

That was one of the hardest things I'd ever done. I hated sharing this, but the one thing that I've learned through this healing process is this: once you speak something out to another person, the hold it has on you is gone.

"Therefore confess your sins to each other and pray for each other so that you may be healed. The prayer of a righteous person is powerful and effective." James 5:16

A secret sin can't control you any longer once you tell another. I honestly don't know that I would label this a *secret sin,* but I do know it had a terrible hold on me that was broken once I *spoke it out.*

After we talked, I had the most amazing experience. I was sitting in my office and I started thinking about the statement *You were supposed to be a boy* and wham, this huge wave of disappointment hit me and I started sobbing, and the thought *I've been a disappointment since the day I was born* kept running through my mind.

Then very clearly, I felt God reveal to me, *No, you are not a disappointment.* And then I felt like I was choking. It felt like something was actually being pulled out of me.

I know this sounds a bit weird. Okay, I'll say it for you, it sounds downright crazy. But it's what happened, I am not kidding, nor am I exaggerating. It was awful. I could barely breathe; it got so intense, and I was just about hyperventilating. I had no idea what was happening to me or what to do.

I began to pray and all of a sudden it seemed like I heard the words, *It's finished.*

And no, there was no booming voice behind me; it was more like the words were inside of me. God has never spoken aloud to me as he did to Moses, but his spirit resonates loud and clear in my soul when he reveals truth. This day was no different.

The choking sensation stopped, my breathing resumed a normal rhythm and I lay there, befuddled by what had just occurred. As I rested, the peace that can only come from the Holy Spirit filled my soul, replacing that abyss that the lies had previously inhabited.

I spent quite a bit of time thinking about what I had experienced, and I began to wonder how many others might have these same thoughts?

How many poor women and men are in the world, thinking that they are of the wrong gender, and doing all sorts of crazy things to themselves and their bodies because they think they are a mistake?

Newsflash: God doesn't make mistakes!

But if they are believing the lie, they are being deceived. I actually saw a special on television one night about very young children believing they were the wrong gender and actually going through a process to change themselves into someone else.

It broke my heart to see this; many of them have actually undergone medical procedures to enable this process to occur. They were actually mutilating the bodies that God gave them to become someone else.

I don't profess to be a psychiatrist or psychologist, nor do I claim to understand all the workings of the human mind. I don't profess to have supernatural knowledge of why people are the way they are. I do not have all the answers, but I have to question this. Maybe someone else's situation is like mine; maybe they are simply believing the lie. Maybe if they found truth, the lie would vanish.

I wonder how many people who profess the gay lifestyle are really simply mixed up souls who have a lie stuck inside of them that they've never been able to break free from?

I know this is a very sensitive area. But I believe it is vital to discuss.

I shared my story one day with a friend. I wasn't sure while I was telling it, why I was even sharing it with her; it was not a comfortable story for me to tell. I had never shared it openly before, but I knew when I ended why she was hearing it.

As I told her my tale, her eyes got wider and wider until she finally blurted out, "My sister is just like you."

She then proceeded to tell me the story of her sister, who was called a tom boy all her life, and at the age of thirty-four, decided that she was gay. And she was miserable and depressed and no one knew how to help her.

But after my friend heard my story, she was encouraged to go talk to her sister, and share another side of the equation with her. And maybe, just maybe, the lie would be unveiled.

God has a wonderful plan for each person. He knew even before He created this world what beauty He would bring forth from our lives.

—Louis B. Wyly

God Has a Plan

"For I know the plans I have for you, declares the
LORD, plans to prosper you and not to harm you,
plans to give you hope and a future. Then you will call
upon me and come and pray to me, and I will listen to
you. You will seek me and find me when you seek me
with all your heart. I will be found by you, declares the
LORD, and will bring you back from captivity."
Jeremiah 29:11-14

Today I was given the opportunity to share my story with a group of women during their monthly meeting. I didn't count how many were there, but I would venture to say there were eighty to ninety women; it was a pretty large organization. They had a meeting about 11:00 a.m., followed by a missionary speaker, then lunch time. After lunch, there were two more speakers—myself and a lady who writes children's books. It was a full schedule. I ended up being the last speaker of the day, and by the time I stood up to speak, I really thought the ladies might be tired and their attention waning.

I was quite pleased to discover though, as I started sharing my story, that all eyes were on me and their interest stayed focused on what I was saying. Those ladies sat for another thirty minutes, totally engrossed in hearing what Jesus has done in my life. As I talked, I could see God working in their hearts, eyes would tear over and tissues were being pulled out of purses.

When I finished speaking, the ladies gathered around me, encouraging me and thanking me for sharing my heart and opening up my life to them. Several talked of daughters and granddaughters who had experienced similar situations as mine.

When I got home, I was relaying to one of my online groups, who I had asked earlier to pray for me, how the meeting went. I mentioned to them how neat it was that God could take my rotten, sinful past and turn it into a message of healing and hope for others who are hurting. One of the girls replied back, "Who would've known that even when you were making bad choices, God had a plan! Wow, that alone is so comforting!"

You know, sometimes when life is going great, it's easy to see God's hand at work in or through us. But how many times, when our life is a *mess*, do we say, "Hey, God's really doing something here!"? What a comfort to know that even in the midst of chaos, God's plan is at work!

———————

Father, I thank you for the opportunity to share my story with those beautiful women. Father, thank you for giving me the words that they needed to hear, the words that touched their hearts, the words that encouraged them to come over and share their stories with me. Father, everything hidden must come to light. No wound can heal when it is covered. Thank you for healing my heart, Lord, and I pray that hearts are continually touched by you and healing follows.

I Love You Jesus.
In Your Name I Pray,
Amen

God's promise for today:

*"I press on to take hold of that for which Christ Jesus
took hold of me. Brothers, I do not consider myself yet
to have taken hold of it. But one thing I do: Forgetting
what is behind and straining toward what is ahead,
I press on toward the goal to win the prize for which
God has called me heavenward in Christ Jesus."
Philippians 3:12b -14*

*"Therefore, I urge you, brothers, in view of God's
mercy, to offer your bodies as living sacrifices, holy and
pleasing to God—this is your spiritual act of worship.
Do not conform any longer to the pattern of this
world, but be transformed by the renewing of your
mind. Then you will be able to test and approve what
God's will is—his good, pleasing and perfect will."
Romans 12:1, 2*

*"God can do anything, you know—far more than you could
ever imagine or guess or request in your wildest dreams!
He does it not by pushing us around but by working
within us, his Spirit deeply and gently within us."
Ephesians 3:20, 21 (MSG)*

*"Let us run with endurance the race that is set before us,
looking unto Jesus, the author and finisher of our faith."
Hebrews 12:1, 2 (NKJV)*

The Lies of Fear— The Sting of Death

Death has always troubled me. My first encounter with it was when one of my favorite uncles died when I was about fourteen years old. He was diagnosed with Aplastic Leukemia and was gone within the year.

I remember looking at his wax-like body at the funeral home and he looked so much like my dad and it petrified me that it could have been my father up there, stiff and still and gone from this world.

I couldn't imagine being placed in a box and buried deep under the ground. Although I knew that a dead person has no knowledge of what is going on, it still freaked me out.

On top of that scenario, I was scared to death to go to hell. Now, why I just didn't turn my life over to the Lord and eliminate that fear makes no sense to me at all...now. But once again I have to say this, when you are believing lies, you are deceived. Your actions don't make sense, because your life is lived through a veil of deception.

So I went through my life praying that I would not die before I gave my life to Jesus. Yes, I did pray throughout my life, even though I didn't really believe that God would hear me. I would never acknowledge his sovereignty in my life, but I continued to pray in my odd, not believing sort of way.

And God answered that prayer. I did come to know him as my Lord and my Savior; he spared my life so many times.

There were several times during my years without Jesus that I wanted to take my own life, but I never followed through with it, I believe mainly because of this deep-seated fear of death. And although I didn't want to live any longer, I was more fearful of death, so in the end life always won out.

As rotten as it was, as hopeless as I felt, that fear inside of me was stronger than any other emotion. In looking back, I have to say, in this instance, I'm glad fear won out. I am glad I was too scared of death to end my life.

I am here today to share these revelations with you and my prayer in doing so is that you will find hope and healing as well, through a personal relationship with Jesus Christ, who died so that you might live.

Recently, I once again came face to face with this fear of death: there was no more hiding from it. It hit me full force. I was at church one morning when my cell phone rang. It was a detective, trying to reach Bobby. She was looking for next of kin to David Schneider. When I was able to reach Bobby, my question to him was,

"Bobby, what happened to David?" I had asked the question, but I was not prepared for the answer.

"He was killed last night on his motorcycle," Bobby whispered back to me.

Oh no, I thought. *No, not David.*

Bobby's brother, David, was two years older than Bobby, a year younger than me. He moved to Naples the year we built our home and lived with us that first year.

He left our house and moved into a hotel several months later; his company was paying, so why not? David would come to dinner every Wednesday night, whether we invited him or not. But, David was always a welcome guest, and he always cleaned his plate; he loved to eat, especially when Bobby was cooking.

As he settled into his new life in Naples, we'd see him less and less, but he was always around for holidays, and we'd catch up on his life.

Our first Thanksgiving with our little Carson included Bobby and I, Carson, Aunt Jane (my sister), and Uncle David. It was a nice little family gathering and we enjoyed each other's company. And our little family settled into a holiday tradition for years to come.

In the early morning hours of February 24, 2007, David made a poor decision that ended in his death, and Bobby and I seemed to be left to put the pieces of his shattered life into some sort of semblance.

We went to the scene of the accident, and stood looking at the road where he crashed. There was a small skid mark down the middle, an oil leak on the side, some chipped pavement; not many clues to let us know what happened that dark night before.

As we walked into his house, I expected to see him sitting on the couch watching a race on TV. After all, it was Sunday afternoon. But the giant screen television was silent.

The only sound was the sobbing of his girlfriend, as she clutched a couple of his t-shirts to her swollen eyes.

As we wandered around the house, Bobby and I kept looking at each other, thinking, *Is this it? Is this all there is?* And for David, the answer was a very real, very sad…yes.

We went about the next few days, doing the things that needed done. It was odd, steaming the clothes that he was going to be buried in, picking out music for the service, planning who was to say what at the funeral.

On the day of the service, we talked to the boys and

explained to them what was about to happen and tried to prepare them, but nobody prepared *me*. As I walked up to his coffin, my heart stopped beating for a second.

I took a deep breath. Ahhhhh…David.

I then turned and smiled at the people who came to say their goodbyes and tried to make them feel comfortable in a place that was oh so very uncomfortable to oh so many.

It was a nice service, as far as services go. I think David would have been okay with it. It was a little difficult to pick out the music, as I really didn't think Led Zeppelin and Black Sabbath would be appropriate at the church, so we settled for Harry Chapin and Eric Clapton. And it worked.

When we got home, Bobby pulled me aside and started telling me stories of what had really happened to David the night he died. Apparently David's friends knew a little bit more about that evening, than the police had shared with us. As his words permeated my mind, I could feel my world start to flip.

By the way, did I mention that I'm not good with blood or injuries? One time I fainted when Bobby came home from work with a bandaged hand. Another time, I slammed my hand in a sliding glass door, and I was down for the rest of the night. I have lots of fainting stories. It's the way God made me. I've been fainting since I was a little kid.

Well, Bobby started telling me what had happened to David and down I went.

Bobby should have known that I couldn't handle this information, and I should have stopped him from telling me, but he needed someone to talk to and I was it.

The picture in my mind, of David, on his motorcycle, zooming through the darkness, and then crashing into the back of the three-wheel trike in front of him at a speed of over 100 mph was implanted in my mind. I tossed and turned all night; I just could not sleep. About dawn I dozed off, only to be awakened by Chase climbing into my bed at 7:15 a.m. to snuggle. *Oh no, we're late* was my thought as I stumbled up.

I staggered into the kitchen, trying to shake the nightmares from my mind. *I'll get the boys breakfast quickly and get them off to school. They have testing and can't be late.*

I opened the freezer to pull out the waffles and I was met with an empty box. *Oh … okay, no problem, I'll make French toast.* As I reached for the bread wrapper, my hand pulled out an empty bag.

I have nothing to fix them for breakfast, shattered across my mind and I just seemed to melt into a puddle on the kitchen floor, sobbing uncontrollably.

I can't even feed my children, was all that would register in my mind. My brain wasn't functioning and I could not stop crying, nor could I pull myself together. I just sat there sobbing with pictures of David's mangled body flashing through my mind.

Then, through the fog, I realized I needed help. I could not let the boys see me like this. I had to get myself together; I needed prayer. I pulled myself up, grabbed the phone and dialed my friend, Miss Cindy.

"Please pray," I sobbed, when her cheery voice answered. And pray she did. Those words of encouragement and hope permeated through my fog, and slowly my sobs subsided. Where there was no rhyme or reason, the prayers of my friend penetrated the darkness.

When she realized that the Lord had calmed me, she encouraged me to get the boys up and get them off to school and then to call her back and let her know how I was doing.

I got the boys up, found a forgotten box of Pop Tarts, and headed out the door, they had breakfast to go.

I was heading down the boulevard towards school when I looked in the rear view mirror, and there was a Harley, roaring up behind me. It gave me a such a start! The images of David's horrible accident flashed back in my mind.

No Lord, I cried, *I can't go there.*

But the damage was done and bit by bit my emotions started slipping and sliding away from the reality I knew.

I knew in my heart that I was okay, Bobby was okay, and the boys were okay. But in my mind, the enemy had planted his lies of deception.

What if something happened to Bobby now? What if something happened to the boys?

What if something happened to me?

I'd be driving along, and a car would come up on me, and I'd start to panic. I saw motorcycles everywhere, and they would always send me back to the memory of David, his still body lying in that coffin.

On my courier route, every time I went to the hospital, the sight of an empty stretcher would bring pictures of David's mangled body to my mind.

I would drive down the road where his accident occurred, expecting to come upon him lying there crumpled in the dirt.

I would fight the mental pictures. I would rebuke the scenes. I would ask God to take them away. I would deny what was happening inside.

I love the Lord. He is my life. David's death could not be affecting me this way.

But there was no denying the anxiety that was rising up inside of me, intensifying on a daily basis.

I had previously experienced a huge challenge while driving, but I had gotten free of it. But during this time, all the peace I had obtained while driving was gone. Driving once again became torturous—I would see cars crashing into me or me becoming distracted and crashing into them.

I would continually tell myself, *Joyce, do not go by your feelings, go by what you know.*

My mind kept replying, *But you know you shouldn't be feeling so out of control. It's not right.*

And I wasn't right.

But I didn't want to talk to anyone about it. I saw it as a sign of weakness, and I didn't want anyone to know I was weak and struggling.

Good grief, I thought, *I write books about my relationship with Jesus. I talk to people all over the country about all the wonderful things he's done for me. And now, my brother-in-law, who I was not even that close with, dies, and I fall apart?*

What sort of testimony is that?

One night, I went to my Tuesday night ladies study, and I sat there and looked around the room, and I could not talk. I could not enjoy the lesson. I wanted to run away. I didn't belong there. All those crazy thoughts of years before started welling up and over-powering me, but I kept trying to push them away.

I did belong there; these were my Bible girls, my friends. At the end of the study, I asked for prayer, because I was to speak the next night, and I was wondering how I was going to stand up in front of a group of teens and share Jesus when every time I opened my mouth, I wanted to cry.

I didn't tell them why I wanted prayer. I didn't explain what was going on inside of me. I couldn't talk about it, because I didn't know what *it* was.

The next morning, I woke up to an email from my friend wanting to know if I was okay because I had been very quiet the night before.

It would have been easy to say, "I'm *fine*," and make up some excuse, but I knew I had to admit the truth. I wasn't fine. I didn't know what was going on inside of me, but I knew something wasn't right.

We met for lunch, and although she tried to encourage me, I just could not shake the discouragement and depression that kept invading my heart.

At one point during our lunch, I had to look away from her, I could not stop the tears that were welling up, and the sadness was overwhelming. The worst part of it was that I could not explain any of it. I did not know why I was being affected this way or what was going on inside of me?

Why did I feel like I was spinning out of control?

She was extremely concerned and made me promise to go home and get under my quillow, my place of refuge; the place where I find my comfort in Jesus—the place where his peace always finds me.

I took her back to work and headed home, determined that Satan was not going to steal my joy, or rob me of my peace another day.

I got home and headed straight for my prayer room. The tears poured down my face as I poured out to Jesus all the hurt that was building up inside. I literally begged him for his peace.

And then I lay silent, waiting on him. And as I lay there, I very clearly heard the words deep within my soul: the *wages of sin are death*.

Yes, I knew that, but there was something very clear and very finite when Jesus shared this statement with me. The words didn't scare me or freak me out. In fact, they brought a calmness to my spirit.

David was dead. There was nothing I could have done to prevent it or change it. He was gone. I didn't need to relive that horrible night again and again, hoping that somehow, it could have had a different ending. It was finished.

But my life with Jesus, that was just beginning. There is so much hope in a life filled with him.

My world had been spinning out of control, but as I lay there, resting in his peace, it seemed like he actually reached down, picked me up off that spinning saucer, and placed me right in the palm of his hand.

I was safe.

When I realized that the spinning had stopped, I opened my eyes and looked through the curtains of my room, and I saw the trees outside. I saw the birds flying. I saw the sun light.

Then, I felt like he was saying to me, *This is life—you chose life*!

Oh… my! Yes, I did. I chose Jesus.

The lies of the enemy were gone. God's truth had pushed them out of my mind and out of my heart.

I got up, and I walked into a room of teenagers that night and told them about what it means to have a personal relationship with a loving caring Savior who loves us so much, who meets us just where we are, who gave his life so that we could live with him forever…if we would only *choose* him.

My prayer for you today is choose life! There is so much hopelessness in this world, so much death and destruction. But look outside your window. Look at the trees, or the mountains, the birds or the beach and know that God loves you and he so desires to give you life through his son, Jesus Christ!

> Our days are numbered. One of the primary goals in our lives should be to prepare for our last day. The legacy we leave is not just in our possessions, but in the quality of our lives. What preparations should we be making now? The greatest waste in all of our earth, which cannot be recycled or reclaimed, is our waste of the time that God has given us each day.
>
> —Billy Graham[3]

Waking Up With God

"Yea, though I walk through the valley of the
shadow of death, I will fear no evil: for thou art
with me: thy rod and thy staff they comfort me."
Psalm 23:4

I wanted to share a thought from Chase about his version of death—his is much more peaceful than mine. Carson and Chase had never been to a funeral service before, and although we really weren't sure what their reaction would be, they loved their Uncle David, and we wanted them to be there to say goodbye, to help them understand the death process a little better. Although I have to confess, I don't know how I could expect them to understand it when I didn't.

On the way home I could tell Chase was thinking; he was very quiet. And then all of a sudden he said, "When I die, I just go to sleep, right Mommy? And then when I wake up, my spirit is in heaven with God. Right?"

Bless his little heart. I could tell he was trying to fit this *death thing* into something that he could handle. And he could handle going to sleep and waking up with God.

As I shared with you previously, death held so much pain and confusion and fear for me. It was a battle that I had to work through intensely to find peace, but not Chase. God gave my little man sweet insight into what happens when you die and you've given your life to Jesus.

Your body is gone, but your spirit wakes up with Him! I wish it hadn't taken me so long to grasp this truth. I want to be more like my little Chase when I grow up!

———————————

Lord Jesus, thank you for bringing insight into Chase's heart so that he understands that death may be the end of life here on earth, but it is just the beginning of our eternal life with you!

I Love You Jesus.
In Your Name I Pray,
Amen

God's promise for today:

"For the wages of sin is death, but the gift of God is eternal life in Christ Jesus our Lord."
Romans 6:23

"Jesus said to her, 'I am the resurrection and the life. He who believes in me will live, even though he dies; and whoever lives and believes in me will never die. Do you believe this?'"
John 11:25, 26

"Keep yourselves in God's love as you wait for the mercy of our Lord Jesus Christ to bring you to eternal life."
Jude 1:21

"I call heaven and earth as witnesses today against you, that I have set before you life and death, blessing and cursing;

therefore choose life, that both you and your descendants
may live; that you may love the LORD your God, that
you may obey His voice, and that you may cling to Him,
for He is your life and the length of your days; and that
you may dwell in the land which the LORD swore to your
fathers, to Abraham, Isaac, and Jacob, to give them."
Deuteronomy 30:19, 20 (NKJV)

Helping Our Children Remove the Lies

So, I wondered if this praying technique would work on the boys, and one day I was able to find out that, yes, Jesus does speak to the boys, and yes, they could hear and understand him quite clearly. Not sure why I wondered, God hears our prayers and usually little kids are a lot more open than adults, but it was neat to be able to experience the healing process with Carson one evening.

This is the really cool part: when we ask, believing, and we want answers and are willing to listen and receive them, God is right there for us.

"And whatever things you ask in prayer, believing, you will receive."

(Matthew 21:22, NKJV)

God is always there for us, but so many times we don't want to hear the answers. So we don't ask the questions.

I actually had one friend tell me that she didn't pray about certain situations because she didn't want to know the answers.

Sometimes the answers are hard to hear. But going to God and seeking his truth and *receiving* it is something that has held true for me in each and every circumstance, regardless of the degree of difficulty on my part to actually admit and work through the issue.

Every single time I walk in obedience to God's Word, to

his will for my life,—immediately the peace of God fills my heart. And despite the swirling that might be going on out in the world, the peace that has settled into my spirit is my assurance that I'm walking God's path.

There is an old hymn, "Blessed Assurance," and this concept brings it to mind. The words are:

> Blessed assurance, Jesus is mine!
> O what a foretaste of glory divine!
> Heir of salvation, purchase of God,
> born of his Spirit, washed in his blood.
> This is my story, this is my song,
> praising my Savior all the day long;
> this is my story, this is my song,
> praising my Savior all the day long.
> Perfect submission, perfect delight,
> visions of rapture now burst on my sight;
> angels descending bring from above
> echoes of mercy, whispers of love.
> Perfect submission, all is at rest;
> I in my Savior am happy and blest,
> watching and waiting, looking above,
> filled with his goodness, lost in his love.

I love the words in the last verse; perfect submission, all is at rest; I in my Savior am happy and blest.

And that is such an adept description of what occurs in our spirit and in our lives when we submit to God, not because we have to, but because we want to.

God doesn't want us to be puppets on a string. He created us with free will to make our own decisions. That is why it is so very special to him when we willingly choose to obey, when we go against the natural desires of our flesh and walk his way.

My little Carson found this out one night as well. It started out a major battle but oh, the ending was so very sweet.

This particular night, Carson was really having a rough time. He was having a bad day, period. Nothing he did was going right; he was fighting with his brother, with his daddy, and even with our dog Zeke. I have never seen Carson upset with Zeke, even when Zeke has jumped on him and hurt him or scratched him really badly; Carson always lets Zeke off the hook. Zeke is the love of his life.

But not this particular night, even Zeke was on his list. He was not a happy camper.

I was sitting in my office, and I heard Carson and Bobby going at it, and then Carson slammed into the room, threw himself on the bed, and was sobbing hysterically.

Bless his little heart. I felt so sorry for him.

I tried to calm him down, but nothing was working. So I decided I would do for him what I always need when I feel like that; I started praying for him.

I prayed for quite a while and I could sense Jesus working in Carson, and Carson calmed down and was able to share a little with me about why he was so upset. We then prayed about what was upsetting him, and all in all, we spent about an hour praying and talking, and it was a sweet time. And by the time I left the room, Carson was just about asleep, and his sobs had subsided.

He seemed in a much better mood the next morning, and the same held true when he got home from school. I even had to run back into town right after they got home from school, and neither of them like when that happens, especially Carson, but this didn't even cause him to fuss. He just chatted away the entire ride to and from town.

He was pleasant at dinner and pleasant all evening, doing his chores and homework without incident.

When he went to bed, he was lying there with his daddy and Bobby was asking him if he felt better about what was bothering him, and he said yes he did, and then he looked over at me and said, "I'm glad we prayed Mommy. That helped me."

Oh my goodness, what a wonderful testimony of our loving Savior who is always there for us. Who truly does hear our prayers and cares about our hearts and our hurts. Who heals the hearts of ten-year-old little boys and forty-year-old mommies and anyone else who *believes* in him.

The prayer preceding all prayer is, may it be the real I who speaks. May it be the real you that I speak to.

—C. S. Lewis

Clean and Clear

"Search me, O God, and know my heart; test me and know my anxious thoughts. See if there is any offensive way in me, and lead me in the way everlasting."
Psalm 139:23, 24

Every night before the boys go to sleep, I spend a few minutes with them. I lie down beside them; ask them about their day, chat a bit, and then we pray. Afterwards, the lights go out, and off to sleep they go.

In the last section, I shared about the night Carson was having some behavior problems; he was just not himself. As it turned out he had an issue inside that was bothering him. When we got it out, he was back to being Carson again—still an irritant to his brother, but nothing out of the norm for a ten-year-old little boy.

I've taken to asking each of the boys before we pray, "Are you clean and clear?" Do they have anything inside that they want to get out? Or is everything good in their heart?

I spent too much time holding in my junk, and I wasted away too much of my life. I don't want my little guys following my example. If they have something bothering them, I want to encourage them to get it out and get it out immediately.

If they answer yes, we say our prayers and move forward.

If it's no, we ask Jesus to reveal what's bothering them, then we pray for him to show them the truth about what they are feeling and *voila*, the problem is usually gone.

Jesus is all about simple solutions. If we ask, he answers.

So I'll ask you what I ask Carson and Chase each night, "Are you clean and clear?"

Father, thank you for always being there for us, for caring so much about each and every aspect of our lives. Help us to not let those wounds fester inside but to bring them to light so that your truth can heal. Help us to stay clean and clear Lord, so that your light shines brightly through us.

> I Love You Jesus.
> In Your Name I Pray,
> Amen

God's promise for today:

"Ask, and it shall be given to you; seek, and you shall find; knock, and it shall be opened to you."
Matthew 7:7 (NASB)

"The earnest prayer of a righteous man has great power and wonderful results."
James 5:16 (TLB)

"Train up a child in the way he should go, even when he is old he will not depart from it."
Proverbs 22:6

"Let no one look down on your youthfulness, but rather in speech, conduct, love, faith and purity, show yourself an example of those who believe."
I Timothy 4:12

Breaking Vows—
Letting Go ... Letting God

This is a hard story to write. I wonder why I can write and talk about my abortion and my past of drugs, alcohol, and promiscuity without so much as a hiccup, but when I try to write down problems occurring in my life in the here and now, I want to stop and say, "Oh, this isn't really important. This is just everyday stuff. I don't need to share this."

And that is the lie, or at least part of the lie. I do need to share it. It's the little foxes that spoil the vines.

The Word says, "Therefore confess your sins to each other and pray for each other so that you may be healed. The prayer of a righteous man is powerful and effective." (James 5:16)

It's important to confess our sins. Oh, not everyone needs to write them down in a book for the world to read. I'm still asking God why he picked me to be that particular person.

But we do need to make a confession of our misdeeds to another. It's in the speaking it out that is the first step towards healing.

I've been going through a training program for a group called Celebrate Recovery. It is a Christian Twelve-Step Program based on the Beatitudes.

The first step in the program is to step out of denial and

admit you have a problem and that you alone cannot solve it.

Principal One: Realize I'm not God. I admit that I am powerless to control my tendency to do the wrong thing and that my life is unmanageable.

"Happy are those who know they are spiritually poor." (Matthew 5:3)

"I know that nothing good lives in me, that is, in my sinful nature. For I have the desire to do what is good, but I cannot carry it out." (Romans 7:18)

So, I go into this program really not thinking about any issues that I still might be carrying inside of me. (This was my first mistake.) I feel like I am taking this class for one reason: so that I can facilitate a group eventually, hoping to focus on women suffering from Post Abortion Syndrome.

I feel like I've pretty much got my stuff under control. But as I sit through a couple of these classes, the questions that we go over in the small group starts to stir up my spirit. I become uncomfortable during these sessions and end up leaving each week agitated, yet unsure about where the agitation is coming from.

I couldn't decide if I was to answer the discussion questions from the viewpoint of where I was when I was struggling through certain addictions or hang-ups. Or what was going on in my life at the present time. And if I answered honestly, the struggles seemed to be focused in on my present circumstances, not my past situations.

But I didn't want to discuss my present concerns. I felt like I was supposed to have it *together,* and how could I sit and confess to this group that I was struggling terribly with financial burdens?

It was a weight that was just about as heavy on me as that horrible burden of abortion had been, if not more so.

Because I knew in my heart that it was not right to carry such debt, yet for whatever reason, I just couldn't seem to get out from under it.

And to make things worse, for years I had been the one in our home who manages the finances, and obviously I had not done a very good job of it, and thus I had to admit another character flaw: I was a failure at managing money.

Oh, I didn't really waste money or spend it foolishly. The main problem was that I had not worked a steady job for ten years, and trying to run a household on one income just hadn't worked out so well for us.

Bobby had given up his career as a chef when Chase was a baby. The hours were not conducive to being a dad, so he had stepped down from that field and went into the construction industry. But in doing so, he went from the top of one vocation level to the bottom of another. And his paycheck went down accordingly.

Now, my wonderful husband had worked his way up through the construction field and made a good income at that point in time, but the damage was done.

In my thinking that the light at the end of the tunnel was just around the corner, I ended up letting debt get way out of control. And I was afraid to tell Bobby just how bad it had become.

A couple of years back we experienced this same scenario, and we put a band-aid on the issue, but I had never actually turned the finances over to Bobby. He didn't really want to be bothered with them, and I had allowed him not to be.

But in doing so, I was dishonoring God and actually dishonoring my husband. He needed to be aware of where our money was and wasn't going. He needed to be the head of the household, whether he really wanted that position or not. It was his God given place of authority, and I had taken it away from him.

Now I didn't mean to take anything away from him, I just didn't want him to know how bad things were and get mad at me for messing them up. But in trying to keep peace, I was going against God's will for our family.

And as I've learned, time and time again, and *always* the hard way, we cannot go against God's will and keep peace in our lives.

I kept feeling like there was something I needed to say during the discussions at group each week, but I didn't want to share this information with the group, or with anyone else, for that matter. My goodness, once again, I didn't even want to share it with my husband. Seems like that is my pattern … as much as I try not to revert to it, once again I was hiding the truth from the one person who needed to know.

You would have thought I'd learned my lesson with the abortion issue, but this is actually part of the problem. This is actually one of the reasons why the information in this book is so vital to understand.

I was believing a lie; so therefore, I didn't realize the damage that I was doing to myself or to our marriage.

Webster calls deception "a misleading falsehood."

When a person falls into deception, they are believing the lie. And so even though they may be aware that something is wrong, they don't know how to make it right. That veil of deception is covering their mind, hindering clear thinking.

Let me share with you this story so you see how danger-ous this can become.

I had been feeling unsettled inside ever since the Cele-brate Recovery Program started. I was the one who encour-aged my friends to come and said that it was a good train-ing for anyone to go through, that we all had stuff that needed to come out.

And sure, that was easy for me to say, for I thought all my stuff was out. That I could just coast through the training and then start doing what I really wanted; help-ing others, facilitate a group. I didn't need it for me, or so I thought…

Okay, so maybe, I knew some little splinters might need pulled out, but I had no clue that there was a giant log in my eye.

One morning, I woke up in the midst of a giant funk. I wasn't sure what was going on inside of me, but I'd been feeling unsettled inside for several weeks. I grabbed my favorite praise and worship CDs for my day of driving, but nothing seemed to be able to pull me out of the pit I felt myself sliding into. I was having the strangest thoughts; maybe I'd pull into The David Lawrence Center, a local men-tal health and substance abuse treatment center, and com-mit myself, so I wouldn't have to deal with my life for a week or two. Or maybe I'd just run the car into a tree, so I wouldn't have to deal with anything ever again.

Those thoughts were really unsettling to me. Where in the world did they come from? I'd immediately push them aside and sing a little louder. But the heaviness would not lift, and by three o'clock in the afternoon, I knew I needed some help and quickly. I could not believe how fast I was falling. It was like days of my past when I drowned myself in alcohol or numbed my reality with pills when life wasn't going my way.

It wasn't drugs or alcohol this time, it was a depression that had fallen upon me, and it was weighing me down in a very unnatural way. I didn't like it, but I seemed powerless to make it stop it. I prayed and prayed that day, but nothing was lifting the burden.

And then I found myself around the corner from Cindy's office, and I knew I needed to stop in a minute and pray with her. I needed God's covering over me and I needed someone not caught up in this downward spiral to intercede for me—a voice of reason to break through my fog-filled mind.

I gave her a call and asked her to meet me downstairs. She took one look at me and asked me what happened. I said I'd been beaten up. When she asked by whom, my reply was, "Me."

I knew I was doing this to myself, but for whatever reason, I seemed unable to stop it. And that was causing me even more distress, because *why* was I letting this happen to me? I knew better!

I was beating myself up for letting this funk hit me and I was struggling through the depression—a double whammy, so to speak.

Cindy led me into an unoccupied room and started to pray for me. Immediately God revealed to me what was going on in my spirit. I was feeling overwhelmed by the idea that I had to carry this money burden myself, that it was up to me to fix it.

After a few minutes of prayer, an old vow that I had made, before Carson was born, came to the surface. I so desperately wanted a baby back in those days that I vowed to Bobby that whatever it took *financially* to keep things going, *I* would make sure we were always okay.

Now, that might seem like a positive thing to say, but when we make a vow, we are taking the control of our lives away from God and saying, "Hey, don't worry about this one, I can handle it."

And in the spiritual, it just doesn't work. How many times have you heard a girl say, "I'm never going to be like my mother," and she is. Or a woman may say, "I am never going to let someone hurt me like that again," and she goes through one abusive relationship after another.

In Matthew, Chapter 5, Verses 33-37, Jesus tells us:

> *"Again, you have heard that it was said to the people long ago, 'Do not break your oath, but keep the oaths you have made to the Lord.' But I tell you, Do not swear at all: either by heaven, for it is God's throne; or by the earth, for it is his footstool; or by Jerusalem, for it is the city of the Great King. And do not swear by your head, for you cannot make even one hair white or black. Simply let your 'Yes' be 'Yes,' and your 'No,' 'No'; anything beyond this comes from the evil one."*

By making that vow, so many years ago, I had actually closed the door for God to help Bobby and me with our finances. And things had grown progressively worse through the years.

I tried several work at home businesses, trying to help make ends meet, so I could be home with the boys. As I mentioned before, Bobby went from the top of his career, to the bottom of a new one so that he could be a dad, spending time with his boys during the evenings and weekends.

Now, yes, through the years he did very well in the construction industry. But the years of too much month and not enough money had taken their toll.

As I broke that vow that afternoon, and released the responsibility back to the Lord, I felt my burden lift immediately.

I hugged my friend, wiped my tear stained face, and gathered myself back up to head on my way. Actually, it was almost humorous at that point. I was laughing as I looked at myself in the mirror.

The lid on my coffee cup had leaked that morning and I had coffee stains all over my shirt. My eyes looked like a raccoon, with all the tears, and I had two big buckets of breast tissue samples sitting in the front seat beside me, ready to head to the lab. This was part of my job, picking up lab samples. Usually the samples are small vials of tissue, but today's pickup seemed to be in proportion to my problem.

Boy, I thought, this could be a soap opera or a sitcom, depending on which side of the truth I was on. Earlier, there was not a funny thought in my head, but after I had gotten to the root of the issue, and the lie disappeared, I could truly laugh at myself and my situation.

As I drove home that day, I was praying for God to show me how to release my finances into his hands. I carried this weight for so long, I honestly did not know how to let it go. But I was determined to give it to God.

And then it hit me. I had to give the finances to Bobby. That was what God wanted me to do. Not pretend like there wasn't a problem. Not hide my head in the sand, hoping the problem would vanish.

I had to take action. I had to take a step of faith. I had to give everything over to Bobby.

Oh no, I kept thinking, *What will he say? What will he do? How can I give this to him?* Oh boy, this was really going to rock our world, and I wasn't sure I wanted to go there.

But God knew best.

When Bobby walked in the door that night, I barely let him catch his breath; I knew I had to spill my guts before I chickened out. So many times in the past, I would wait till *just the right moment*, to start a serious conversation. But I knew there would never be a *right moment* for this one, it was now or never, I had to get it out.

"I can't take care of the money any longer, honey; you are going to have to take it over." Okay, well it was out, it was blunt and Bobby was *not* expecting this. But he handled it well. My precious husband just doesn't miss a beat, most days.

"Well," was his reply, "you're not going to like the way things go if I take it over."

My answer to him was that I didn't like the way things were right now. I was desperate, I couldn't do it any longer, and I needed his help.

I did not go to him in anger, but with a broken and contrite spirit. I never knew before I found Jesus what that really meant. I do now, as the Lord has allowed me to experience it, actually quite frequently. I am a slow learner... sometimes.

As we talked it through, I promised him that I would show him everything within the next week, before his next paycheck and when all the bills would come due.

And I walked away, thinking, *well, that wasn't so hard*.

Until the next evening, when I walked in from Bible Study, all proud of myself for my new revelation and there was Bobby, sitting in front of my filing cabinet, which he had moved out of my office and into the kitchen, and he was going through every piece of paper that was in there.

Every check stub, every credit card statement, every receipt, the man missed nothing.

Wait a minute was my initial thought. *What is he doing in my stuff?* But thankfully, God shut my mouth and I said nothing. As I approached him, I could see he was not in a good mood.

He started holding up papers and receipts and questioning me about them. I could feel myself start to explode inside and then very calmly I said, "Honey, you have not been interested in this stuff for the past fifteen years. I have had to take care of it myself. I've done the best I could, but obviously it's not been so great. That is why I need you to take this over. Now please, be very careful the tone of voice you use with me. I have never done anything intentionally to hurt our family."

And I walked out the door and I sat on the front steps and I burst into tears. I asked God to walk with me through this process that I knew I could never get through without him.

My spirit was too independent. *Who did Bobby think he was questioning? How dare he?*

God gently showed me that I needed to respect Bobby, and I needed to support him and that we would walk through this course of action *together.*

I won't go into all the details, but it was amazing how God softened both our hearts. I willingly submitted to Bobby all the money matters. I allowed him to make any decision he deemed best for us, offering a few suggestions but basically just showing him what was what and letting him go from there.

Bobby's heart changed towards me; he was kind and considerate and never made any fuss whatsoever about the money again. He wanted me to use cash and not a debit card, so it would be easier for him to keep track and every couple of days he would check with me to make sure I had money for gas or anything else I might need.

I thought if he knew how far in debt we were, that he would make me stop doing all the things I loved, make me get a *real* job and ask me to stop speaking to women's groups around the state.

I don't make much money when I go share my story of Jesus, and sometimes I sell a few books, and sometimes I don't, but most of the time, I barely break even. But because it's never been about the money to me, it's always been about sharing Jesus, well it just didn't matter.

And although in the past Bobby did question a trip or two that I took that cost more than normal; hotel rooms, and added gas for the long distances, he never said I had to stop doing it, I just assumed *he would if he knew our financial situation.*

We're still in the *working through the process* stage at this point of my story. I wish I had a huge—"Guess what, we're out of debt now" ending, but that just hasn't occurred, yet.

But I can share this with you. The peace that God has given me is just as important. Even though nothing financially has really changed, *everything* has changed. I still look at the bank account on occasion, but it's more out of habit, curiosity than necessity and I no longer spend my days trying to figure out how to make the money longer and the month shorter.

I am working just as hard because it's important for me to do my share, but I don't carry that financial burden any longer.

I do see a light at the end of the tunnel. I know that this isn't a lifetime sentence, now that Bobby is in charge; he is handling this just like he handles every other aspect of his life. With sincere, intense concern, looking into every detail and working through the obstacles. And it's become a challenge to me to see how much money I *can't* spend each week.

I never realized how different it is to only buy things when you have cash in your pocket. I never realized how deceptive even a debit card could be. I knew the money came out of my checking, but it's one thing to swipe a piece of plastic, and it's a whole other mindset to hand over hard earned cash.

Yes, I am sure you are thinking, how nutty is this girl? Why did it take her so long to realize this? I don't have an answer for you. Except that I know God's timing is always right.

I had to be at this place in my life to receive this lesson in finances and who was to be head of our household concerning those finances. Bobby and I needed to be united in this area, and this experience helped us to achieve that purpose.

Prayer is a long-term investment, one that will increase your sense of security because God is your protector. Keep at it every day, for prayer is the key of the day and the bolt of the evening. God is waiting to hear from you.

—Barbara Johnson

The Broken Car

"Be still, and know that I am God."
Psalm 46:10

I had coffee one day with a very dear friend. This special lady has known the Lord for many decades and has a special gift to teach his Word. She is one of those anointed teachers, who brings the stories of the Bible to life. She has been a great encouragement to me through my journey.

We were chatting about the content of one of my books, and there was one point that she asked me to repeat over and over again, the point that is the *key* to my freedom and the *key* to my spiritual growth, *that surrender thing!*

When I finally allowed God to rule over my life, my life started to really change. God could actually give me the blessings that he has for me, the ones that I could never receive before, because I was too busy always trying to do it all myself.

I've discussed with you this point throughout these chapters, but for my dear friend, Miss Jo, and for your benefit, so that I am sure you really understand, I am going to expound upon this topic one more time. I think this story will help you see it more clearly; I know it opened my eyes. And once again, the lesson came from the boys. I love how God uses the boys to make his concepts clear to me.

One day Chase had taken apart his favorite Erector Set

car, and he just could not get it back together again. He asked Bobby to help him with it.

"Sure, Chase," Bobby said. "Leave it here with me, and I'll have it good as new for you in no time."

Bobby was making some crosses at the time, another one of his hobbies, so he set the car to the side, planning on putting it back together after he wrapped a few crosses.

Chase ran into his room to play, but was back in about two minutes and saw that Bobby hadn't fixed the car yet. He picked it up and said he'd fix it himself. He took it into his room and fiddled with it for a bit, and then, defeated by his inability to fix it, brought it back out to Bobby. He admitted that he couldn't fix it and asked Bobby to help him, again.

Bobby readily agreed, but again, before he could begin fixing the car, Chase came back out a second time, impatient that the car wasn't fixed yet, grabbed it off the table again and started working on it himself.

This went back and forth for quite some time, until finally Bobby said, "Chase, I cannot fix your car if you keep taking it back. Please, if you want me to fix it, leave it alone!"

Boy, remember that light bulb going off in the cartoons? I sometimes have a hard time understanding *how* to surrender something to God. I didn't realize the concept of giving it to him and then taking it back upon myself, because I was trying to help him or because I was impatient. However, this illustration made it oh so very clear to me.

Chase was not only taking the car away so that Bobby could not fix it, but in the process, he was making it worse with all his fiddling. In spite of his good intentions, he was making it impossible for Bobby to help him. When Chase finally set the car on the table and walked away, keeping his hands off it, then, and only then, could Bobby fix the problem for him.

Ouch...how many times have I *given* my situations to the Lord, only to come back the next day and decide he really needed my help keeping things running smoothly? I would give him an issue, and no sooner would I say it was up to him than I'd snatch it back because things weren't moving as fast as I'd like them to. I could take care of it quicker myself. It was all about my timing...*not God's.*

I had to take my hands off my *broken life* and walk away and stay away to allow God to do his thing. But oh, the life he has made for me since then is so much more than I could have ever imagined! That abundant life that can only come through Jesus Christ!

═══════════════

Father, this is such a wonderful analogy of what my life looks like when I keep taking back the things that I should give to you and leave with you. Thank you for giving me these stories, to show me clearer and to help others see you in a way that they can understand as well. Father, help me to continue to let go and let you!

> I Love You Jesus.
> In Your name I pray,
> Amen

God's promise for today:

> *"The Lord longs to be gracious to you; he rises to show you compassion. For the Lord is a God of justice. Blessed are all who wait for him!"*
> *Isaiah 30:18*

"Our help is in the name of the Lord,
who made heaven and earth."
Psalm 124:8

"Faith by itself, if it is not accompanied by action, is dead."
James 2:17

"Let him have all your worries and cares,
for he is always thinking about you and
watching everything that concerns you."
I Peter 5:7

The Lie of Failure—
The Face in the Mirror

In the middle of learning this financial lesson, God brought another lesson into my life. I am not really sure I've ever had two or more lessons going on at the same time, so it took me a little bit longer to grasp the second one.

Right about the time I turned the money matters over to Bobby, I started feeling *different* inside. Now, I know that we are not to gauge our life by our feelings. We've discussed this before. But this was not some emotional fixation that I was experiencing but rather an emptiness that seemed to settle into my spirit.

I didn't really pay a lot of attention to it at first; I chalked it up to my going through this huge change in our financial roles. I was no longer *in charge*. I didn't have to be *the one* taking care of everything. I figured that probably the change in roles was the reason I felt so different.

And I was okay with it. But then one night something happened that stopped me cold in my tracks. I have experienced enough of inner healing and spiritual warfare and flesh issues and spiritual issues to realize that something was not right.

As I've said before, I don't always know *what's wrong*, but I always know when something isn't *right*.

I follow my peace, and although I had total peace about

turning the finances over to Bobby, my spirit seemed to be lacking something; there was no joy in my day to day life.

Nehemiah 8:10 says, "The joy of the Lord is your strength." Ummmm...well that was true. I always attributed my joy to the Lord. So, if my joy was gone, did that mean the Lord was gone?

No, that's impossible. In Deuteronomy 31:6, Moses told the Israelites, "Be strong and courageous. Do not be afraid or terrified because of them, for the LORD your God goes with you; he will never leave you nor forsake you."

So, in my head I knew that the Lord would never leave me, but why did I feel that emptiness that I had fought so long against, the emptiness that always seemed to want to sneak back in just when I was least expecting it?

And of course, that brings me right back to our enemy, Satan. He is the master of deception. He loves to mess with our lives, to throw a wrench into the gears of our spirit, to keep our focus off of Jesus and on to ourselves and our problems.

Joanna Weaver discusses this concept in her book, *Having a Mary Heart In a Martha World.*

I love how she puts it:

> Satan's never been terribly creative. The tools he uses today are the same tools he's always used—and no wonder, for they've been quite effective from the Garden of Eden, to Martha's Bethany kitchen to our own everyday world, Satan still plans his attacks around what I call the "Three Deadly Ds of Destruction."
>
> They are
> •Distraction
> •Discouragement
> •Doubt

> Throughout time, Satan has resorted to these tactics to bring down God's best and brightest. The underlying strategy is simple: Get people's eyes off God and on their circumstances. Make them believe that their "happiness" lies in the "happenings" that surround them. Or send them good news—about somebody else. When they're thoroughly discouraged, tell them God doesn't care. Then sit back and let doubt do its work.
>
> It's really a brilliant strategy, when you think of it. Plant the Deadly Ds deep in human hearts, and sooner or later people will destroy themselves.
>
> Unless, of course, someone intervenes—which is exactly what Jesus came to do.[4]

I was struggling with all three of the Deadly D's; I was being deceived, in a big way. In the midst of working through the financial challenges with Bobby, I was also struggling with some issues at my church. The issues were not theology based, just personality differences. Community can be messy. I was trying to learn how to work well with others, a lesson I should have learned in Kindergarten. I wasn't sure why the challenges were overwhelming me, but it seemed like every time I would put out one fire, another would pop up. Working with people is a blessing. Working with people can be a challenge, whichever way you want to look at it. At this point in my life, the challenges seemed to be winning, and I was losing my peace, big time.

It was getting the best of me; I became discouraged and ready to throw in the towel. Not with God. But a thought did cross my mind that I could go to the big church down the street and get lost in the midst of the thousands of nameless faces and remove myself from the stress of being on the front line, so to speak.

There is never a dull moment in my world. But I have learned through the lessons that if it were dull and boring, I probably wouldn't be much of a threat to Satan—he'd just leave me alone. And I want to be a threat to him. I want him concerned about what I'm doing because my desire is to share Jesus with everyone I encounter. I want to be the kind of woman that when my feet hit the floor in the morning the devil says, "Oh boy, she's up!"

But during this time I wasn't really feeling like such a threat … I was feeling empty and discouraged.

So, I'm thinking that the emptiness is due to the change in roles at home, but then one night, I am walking past my mirror and I look at myself and what popped into my head really scared me.

I thought, *Well, I still look like me.*

Now, why in the world would I be thinking something like that? But it wasn't even the thought that got to me. It was the way I looked at myself. Like I was seeing me in the mirror, but I could not relate myself to that person inside.

This is so odd, was my next thought. *What in the world have you done now Joyce,* came shortly after.

Now, I really don't know why I thought I had *done* anything. But I was and am so used to me messing up, that I take it for granted mostly now. I know that is a wrong thought, I know I don't *always* mess up, but what you just heard was the deception. The lie. And when we believe something, we don't know it's a lie. We think it's truth. Hence, we are deceived.

I was heading to bed when I had these thoughts, and I almost jumped up and emailed Cindy. I always run this stuff by her; she has way more wisdom in this area than I do, not to mention she is the detached third party who can help me see more clearly through the fog.

She has a gift of discernment, and I've learned through the years that she will speak truth to me. I may not always like to hear what she says, but I always know its truth and it's for my own good.

But I was tired, and I didn't want to get back up, and I thought, oh, I'll tell her tomorrow when I see her. We'd be at study together; I'd try to find a minute to share this new thought that was cruising through my brain.

Why did I feel so different inside that I was surprised to see that I still looked the same on the outside?

After our study time, I did share the thought with her, and she agreed that it was an odd thing to think, but maybe I *was* experiencing some sort of identity crisis now that Bobby was stepping into his role as the head of our household.

She suggested I do what I always do when I don't know; get under my quillow and ask God. He has all the answers, and if we are willing to receive them, he's happy to share them with us.

At least the ones he wants us to work on or through. There are some answers I've never received, but with those, I figure he really did give me an answer, it was either "No," or "Not right now."

But when my peace is unsettled, when I'm just not feeling right inside, when I seek out God, he is always there to bring me his truth.

I pondered what was going on all evening and the next day while I was out driving.

A positive aspect of my job is that it gives me a lot of

time to think. A challenge with my job is that it gives me a lot of time to think.

It seemed like I was feeling like I had failed in my duties with my church because of the personality challenges I struggled with. Nothing bad had happened, everything was worked out, but for some reason, I developed an *I don't care* attitude and I wasn't sure why or what to do with it. It was almost like I was forcing myself to even *go to church*, and I'd never experienced that before. I loved being a part of my church family. I honestly would rather be at church than any place else.

That seemed to be the answer to why I didn't feel like *me* any longer because *me loves church!* And when that love went away, who I was went away with it. And I wasn't sure why or what to do about it.

As I pondered the concept a bit, God revealed to me that I was the one who put up the wall. I allowed my feelings to be hurt by others, and in my subconscious, I decided I wasn't going to get hurt any more. If I did not care, it could not hurt me.

But that was what was missing inside of me, the caring, because *I have to care.* It's what drives me: caring about people, caring about things, caring about life.

The more I pondered it the more it seemed like it wasn't so much that I didn't care anymore, it was more the thought, *I give up.* Not *I give up my will, I'm going to let God handle this,* but more the *I quit* sort of proclamation.

I give up didn't seem to be quite the same as *I don't care.* Maybe something else was going on? Inside, I felt like I was a failure. That failure thing was still present and forefront in my emotions. It's been an issue I've struggled with for years.

Not good. And this is the hard part to understand *if* you've never believed a lie.

I knew in my head that I wasn't a failure. I could make a very long list of all my accomplishments. But it wasn't my head that was causing the problems. It was my heart. And in my heart, I *felt* like a failure.

Proverbs 4:23 tells us, "Above all else, guard your heart, for it is the wellspring of life."

It is so important to protect our hearts, at all cost, because once a lie settles in, it poisons our spirit, and we really get into trouble.

I called my friend to talk to her about this emotional rollercoaster occurring inside of me, and she encouraged me to keep pursuing the root of where this failure emotion had started. To ask God to bring to mind any events previously where I had felt I had failed.

I agreed, and let me just interject a thought here. I really have a hard time with people giving me excuses on why they can't find time for healing.

I was in the middle of a busy work day. Driving and working, yet I determined that I was going to let God show me the root of this issue and get it out, *once and for all.*

So, if you have an excuse, please remember, God doesn't want your excuses, He wants your heart.

God obviously wanted me to work through this problem, and yes, I could have put it off by using the excuse I was too busy at the time, but I'm really not sure that would have meshed. I believe when God starts stirring up our insides, it's time to get the lies worked out and if we miss the opportunity, well, we are going to stay stuck even longer.

Once I experienced God's peace, I realized I don't want to ever be without it. I don't even want to go one day struggling through issues. I need him and I'll do whatever it takes to keep myself clean and clear so his spirit flows through me and his peace envelopes me. I used to search for the best high through drugs and alcohol, but I've found that the peace of Jesus surpasses any artificially manufactured high.

As I started praying for God to show me the root of where this all started, my mind went back to a day twenty-five years earlier.

I was driving back to Naples from Daytona Beach, sobbing the entire trip, my heart broken, my life shattered.

I had moved to Daytona with my boyfriend a year and a half earlier, but he decided that he needed his space and he sent me packing back to Naples, pretty much with my tail between my legs.

I had thought we were going to be married and start a family; but he wasn't ready for that commitment.

My heart was broken. I loved him and I blamed myself for our failed relationship. I felt like a failure and I developed an *I don't care attitude* and my life really became crazy from that point forward.

I was having a hard time believing that this incident was really the root, but the more I pondered it, the more intense it became until the thought of that day caused sobs to escape from my heart. It was intensely painful to think about. As I drove around that day, making my deliveries, I was praying and trying to work this thing through and the tears were flowing and my stomach was all knotted up. I would go into an office to pick up or drop off an item, put on my sun glasses, say hello to whomever I met, and then jump back into my car and continue to work through the emotions that kept pouring out of me, with tears flowing freely.

It was not an easy process and it was getting very intense. When something is trying to work itself out, it's not so pretty, and it hurts. Think about how it feels to be in the process of digging a splinter out of your finger—similar illustration. At one point in my day, the pain became quite intense. I pulled my car over to relax a minute. As I sat there staring out my window, my mind kept replaying how abandoned and lonely I felt that day, years earlier when I was driving back to Naples. Even though it had been so many years before, it felt like I was experiencing it *in the moment*. And then the event turned from being abandoned by my boyfriend to being abandoned by Jesus. Why I felt like Jesus abandoned me, I don't know, but what happened next was the most amazing revelation.

It was like Jesus was there with me, in the trees by my car. Not the form of Jesus, they were just regular old palm trees, but it was like his presence was there with me. And he was assuring me that he would never leave me, for he had never abandoned me, and he never would. He loved me. I was his child. It was a pretty intense experience, one of those *wow* moments. And in that instant, immediately the pain of the past was gone and it was replaced with the peace of the Lord!

Truly amazing!

I hadn't even realized it, but when I went through the struggle with my church, I felt like I had failed inside. I felt like I had messed up my one true love and that in doing so, Jesus would abandon me. Now hopefully to make this a little clearer, this was going on in my subconscious, I wasn't aware I felt abandoned. But I knew I felt empty inside, that something was wrong in my spirit.

It was a very difficult revelation, because who wants to

really *admit* that they love Jesus, and yet they feel like he's abandoned them?

In my head, I knew beyond a shadow of a doubt that he would never leave me nor forsake me, but the lie was planted in my spirit, and it was messing up my heart.

Again, the deception of the enemy. If we know what's happening, well, we wouldn't be deceived. But Jesus knew I needed a touch from him that day, and he revealed himself to me in a big way!

Thank you Jesus!

I wish I could explain a little clearer how he revealed himself to me that day, without you thinking I am totally crazy, but I'm not sure I can. God has a way of giving us just what we need, when we need it, and there is no explanation of even how it came about. God knew I needed a touch from him that day, and he gave it to me—pure and simple.

Matthew 21:22 says, "If you believe, you will receive whatever you ask for in prayer."

I believe God's Word!

Once more, lies were removed, truth received, healing occurred.

They who seek the throne of grace
Find that throne in every place;
If we live a life of prayer,
God is present everywhere.

—Oliver Holden

Who Are You?

*"Being confident of this, that he who began
a good work in you will carry it on to
completion until the day of Christ Jesus."*
Philippians 1:6

The other day I was listening to a song by Switchfoot, "This Is Your Life," and the lyrics really stuck in my head. The chorus goes like this:

This is your life, are you who you want to be
This is your life, are you who you want to be
This is your life, is it everything you dreamed that it would be
When the world was younger and you had everything to lose

I kept thinking, *Am I who I want to be? Is my life everything I dreamed about as a kid? Ummmm...?* Good question. As a kid, I used to dream about growing up and having a happy family. I wanted four or five kids, just like my family. But when I grew up, I took a lot of paths that led me into some really bad stuff. A happy family was not on that path. I was on a path of self-destruction.

Then, I did have a family, but it didn't bring me the happiness that I thought it would. Ummmm? That was odd? I had always dreamed that a husband and kids would make me happy. But when I had a wonderful husband and two beautiful little boys, I was still unhappy.

Then one day, I realized that the hole I had been trying to fill all my life, with all the wrong things, was the spot that only Jesus could satisfy. When I finally let him into my life, he healed my heart and my hurts and wiped clean the slate of my past. It was then I discovered true joy in my life, not being merely happy for the moment, but a deep seated peace and joy that can only come from God.

One day I shared my story with a group of ladies. It was a sweet time, and I could see God touching the hearts of those wonderful women.

As I was driving home that day, I was thinking that the question I ask myself shouldn't be, "Am I whom I want to be?" but rather, "Am I becoming the person God made me to be?"

———————

Father, thank you for giving me the opportunity to become the person you want me to be. Lord, I know there have been a lot of detours along the way; I thank you for never giving up on me, even when I've given up on myself. And Father, thank you for giving me the family that is even better than the one I dreamed of as a child.

> I Love You Jesus.
> In Your Name I Pray,
> Amen

God's promise for today:

"And he took them up in his arms, put his
hands upon them, and blessed them."
Mark 10:16 (KJV)

"The Lord is the everlasting God, the Creator of the
ends of the earth. He will not grow tired or weary."
Isaiah 40:28

"I will instruct you and teach you in the way you
should go; I will counsel you and watch over you."
Psalm 32:8

"But the man who loves God is known by God."
I Corinthians 8:3

I'll Never Be Good Enough—The Lie of Deception

It seems like during some seasons of my life I constantly rode a rollercoaster of emotions. But, on a positive note, it was during these challenges that I grew stronger in my faith because God has been faithful to walk with me through these areas of struggle.

Just like the butterfly's strength comes from breaking through his cocoon, my faith has increased as I broke through the layers of lies my heart was encased in. Not skirting around them or trying to ignore them, but actually working through the struggles.

When these lies surface, they usually start out as an innocent thought, but then, just like a splinter will eventually work its way to the skin's surface, as the stirring inside continues, the lie begins to work its way out, if I allow it. I can push it back down and ignore the stirring, but eventually it will work its way back to the surface again. Each time, it's a little more painful, so as hard as this is to believe, I've actually learned to embrace the discomfort, as much as possible, because I know once I get on the other side, the peace will be worth it all.

Faith is made complete when we go *through* the trial. We must press on. We must endure to the end.

We have God's promise:

"But now, this is what the LORD says— he who created you, Jacob, he who formed you, Israel: 'Do not fear, for I have redeemed you; I have summoned you by name; you are mine. When you pass through the waters, I will be with you; and when you pass through the rivers, they will not sweep over you. When you walk through the fire, you will not be burned; the flames will not set you ablaze. For I am the LORD your God, the Holy One of Israel, your Savior.'" (Isaiah 43:1-3)

God didn't promise us no trials, but rather he would be with us as we go *through* them.

It takes more faith to go through the trial, then to go around it. I hope this encourages you when you come face to face with your next trial.

If we stand strong in our faith, we will win. Romans 8:37 says: "Yet in all these things we are more than conquerors through him who loved us."

You may be wondering what all these things are? If we back up to verse 35, we get the answer: "Who shall separate us from the love of Christ? Shall tribulation, or distress, or persecution, or famine, or nakedness, or peril, or sword?"

The bottom line is this, if we walk with Jesus, no matter what is thrown at us, we win. But we have to keep walking.

One morning I was heading up to Englewood to meet with a group of women who were going to host a ladies night out event that I would be speaking at. These events are a time for women to connect, have fun, and hear the message of hope and healing through Jesus.

I showered and fixed the boys breakfast, but upon waking Chase, noticed that he wasn't looking very spry. He'd been up two or three times in the night, which is very unusual. He'd even ended up climbing into bed with Bobby and me. I figured he wasn't feeling so great; I was right.

I laid him on the couch, gave him some medicine, and decided that he'd just have to go with me to the meeting. I'd make him a bed in the car and find him a quiet place to rest at the meeting. No big deal. Chase has been shuttled back and forth his whole life, regardless of how he feels. He even said that day, "I can sleep in the car, Mommy." I have the child trained.

I ended up getting a call from the lady who was hosting the meeting, and when I mentioned to her that I was bringing Chase along, she was a bit concerned about him being contagious. During the process of trying to decide to go or postpone, I took one look at his feverish little face and decided that he didn't need to be dragged all over the country that day; the couch was where he needed to stay.

So, my meeting was postponed. I was a bit disappointed because I was looking forward to talking with the ladies about getting this event together, but I knew there would be another planning meeting soon. It was more important for me to stay home with Chase.

In the middle of the afternoon, the doorbell rang. It was the UPS guy, bringing me boxes of my newest book. I love those days! When I opened that box and saw those books staring up at me I thought, *Wow...it's really here! My new book!*

A book starts out as a virtual thought, usually while I'm driving around, so to actually put my hands on it, admire the cover, leaf through the pages, well, lots of emotions flow and were flowing that afternoon, mostly this thought, *God, You are so cool! Thank You!*

I spent the rest of the day nursing Chase until Bobby came home and relieved me, then off to my Tuesday study I went. I love Tuesday nights with the girls; I have to be out of town or on my deathbed to miss one!

This night was no exception. We were starting a new study, and I was really looking forward to it; plus I had my new book to show the girls.

My friends at study are my support, my rock, and I think they enjoy these new books almost as much as I do.

All was well that night until I got home and an online friend congratulated me on my new book and referred a blog that I should check out by a popular Christian author. The author was giving advice on how to write a book.

I immediately logged onto the blog and started reading. The more I read, the more discouraged I felt. She had all these specifics on how many words your book should be, how many chapters it should be divided into, and a variety of other ideas for how to write a successful book.

As I sat there, reading her information, looking at her picture, visiting other areas of her site, my self esteem seemed to deflate. It was like the air was just pouring out of my balloon.

Who was I trying to fool? I didn't know how to write a book. I didn't have ten topics listed on my website of concepts I could speak on. All I did was stand up there and share my story. Who wanted to hear that? If I were a real speaker, I'd have a whole slew of things that I could talk about, and my calendar would be booked, and...

You get the picture. I was really beating myself up. Then

I closed the website, slammed my computer top down, and sulked off to bed.

I tried to pray about it, but I didn't find any relief. My mind kept replaying the thought *I will never be like those women*. They were all the same; just different names, different ministries, but all with a certain sophisticated look: beautiful hair, perfect nails. They had their pictures taken in dining rooms of homes that looked like they were decorated by Martha Stewart.

I am just a courier, driving around *body parts* all day. I don't even have a tablecloth on my kitchen table and I've never had a pedicure in my life. Jeans, clogs, and sweatshirts are my daily attire.

What was I thinking? I'd never be like them.

These thoughts also seem to haunt me when I look at the website of my publishing company and start viewing the other authors. I don't know anything about these people, yet as soon as I start reading their book descriptions and looking at their covers I think, *I'm not a real author. I don't know why I'm kidding myself. My books are not as good as theirs. I'll never be like them.*

I went to sleep that night, forgetting all the wonderful things God has done for me and my ministry; the four books he allowed me to write; the hundreds of people that I'd been able to share him with, even the daily notes of encouragement I get from others who are blessed by the stories I write. Nope, nothing positive was in my head that night, only the idea that I would never be like those women who had big ministries and spoke to thousands of women at weekend conventions; the women who really knew what they were doing when they wrote a book, the women who were *different* from me.

I woke up the next day determined not to let the emotions of the night before ruin my day, and I was able to push the thoughts back down into that place where I put things I don't want to deal with.

A few days later though, the thought came back to me as I was going through my route. *I am a joke, I am not a real writer*. I called my friend and shared my thoughts with her. As I explained what was bothering me, tears welled up in my eyes, and my throat was all choked, and it was hard to say the words that had been rattling around in my head. She agreed that, "Yes, it did sound like something wasn't quite right inside."

I've said this before but I'll repeat myself so you understand. I do not always know what's wrong, but I *always* know when something is not right. It's not always a clear cut case of a problem, just the concept that things aren't as they should be, in my spirit.

I then started the inward search to find the issue, the root, the lie. When we believe a lie, it distorts reality. I spent enough years living in an alcohol and drug-induced reality. I am not about to let lies sap any more time off my life or the peace that Jesus so readily has for me to embrace.

As I drove that day, I was listening to the radio and David Jeremiah was speaking on how dangerous it is to compare ourselves to others. He finished the message with the statement, "I had to get this clear very early on in my ministry. I was not Billy Graham or any other famous evangelist. I was David Jeremiah."

Those words hit me square in the face. That was just what I had been doing, comparing myself to others. *Okay, Lord*, I said as I flipped off the radio, *I guess it's time to get this out.*

I started praying for God to reveal to me what was causing this inner conflict, what false belief system was messing
with my emotions.

Almost immediately I heard the words, *I'll never be like
them.*

Yep, that was the truth. Just look at yourself, Joyce.
Here you are, driving your little car around town, running
errands, for goodness' sake. You don't have a real ministry.
You're nothing but a delivery girl.

Then I said, "Okay, God. You heard the lie. You know
what's going on. Please, Lord, reveal to me your truth. I
don't want this lie inside of me anymore."

At that moment, I saw myself as God saw me. He
seemed to be saying to my spirit, *I love you! You are so very
special to me. There is no one like you! Look at you!*

Even though I was just driving around town that day
making deliveries in my jeans, clogs, and fleece sweatshirt,
nothing special, just an ordinary day, I immediately felt
extremely special! It didn't matter what I was wearing, or
what I did for a living, God loved me for me! It was like he
was showing me that every part of me was what made me
special, even the way I dress; my crazy lack of style! It was
all a part of me. I was me! He had made me just like this, for
his purpose. I was real. I was unique. I was his child.

It was the neatest feeling. And then, just when I was
thinking, Okay, I am me. I am special, I heard the words, *I
don't want you to be like those other women, I want you to
be you!* Now, just for clarification, I didn't hear the audible
words, like Moses' encounter with God, but I heard them
inside my spirit.

Oh my! I just started laughing! It was the funniest thing
to me. I got a picture in my mind of all those perfectly

coiffed, manicured women, and then there I stood, off to one side in my jeans and sweatshirts, but with the biggest grin on my face because I was up there sharing what Jesus had done for me. And there was nothing more I would rather be doing than sharing his love, his hope, his healing.

I chuckled to myself on and off the rest of the day. I just couldn't stop thinking, *He picked me. He picked me!*

I wrote my first book, not to sell a million copies, but rather to help some poor soul who was suffering the pain of guilt and shame from a past abortion, or maybe a mom who kept having miscarriages and no one seemed to understand her loss or pain. Or for the mom who watched her little stillborn baby get carried away in a pan and wanted to end her own life, because she couldn't stand the reality of losing that precious little baby another day.

I share my story because I know there is always someone listening who needs to hear about the hope and healing that Jesus has for them. I've shared it with four people and I've shared it with five hundred. It never matters to me the number in attendance, but what matters is that a heart is touched by Jesus.

That has been my desire from day one. So why did I think now that if I didn't have some super sized ministry, that I was a failure, that I couldn't be like those who did?

I am me. I will continue to write the lessons that Jesus gives me and I will stand up and share his goodness with whoever he puts in front of me. I will continue to care about others and do all I can to help those who are hurting find hope and healing through him!

God made me this way. I don't want to try to turn myself into some generic somebody, following the crowd. I am unique, created in his image.

"Before I formed you in the womb I knew you, before you were born I set you apart; I appointed you as a prophet to the nations." (Jeremiah 1:5)

This lesson was to fully comprehend who I am, *in Christ,* and learn how to walk in that revelation.

Neil Anderson has written a wonderful book on this subject, *Victory over the Darkness.*

In it he states, "Your hope for growth, meaning and fulfillment as a Christian is based on understanding who you are—specifically your identity in Christ as a child of God."[5]

I would encourage you to read this book. It brought a lot of truths to light for me and helped me to fully understand scripturally what my position as a Christian is. Once I learned who God believes me to be, it became easier for me to believe, and thus begin to walk in that belief system.

We are made for God and nothing less will really satisfy us.

—Brennan Manning

A Sherpa for Jesus

A while back, one of the pastors at church gave a message on *Sherpas*. He had watched a special on television about mountain climbing up Mt. Everest and the Sherpas were the guys in the background who made it possible for the paying customers, so to speak, to make it to the top of the peak. They did all the work behind the scenes, preparing the way for the others. Their lives are based on serving. Just as ours should be, serving for Jesus. It was a wonderful sermon, one I took to heart.

When I started my job as a courier, I decided that while I was out there running errands for the various businesses, I was ultimately being a Sherpa for Jesus. I was ultimately out there to serve him, and every morning before I got in my car, I would ask Jesus to bring the people into my path that He wanted me to meet.

One day I was picking up a package at an office where I've stopped a few times before. Every time I went in, the girl at the front desk would offer me a bottle of water. I guess I always looked dehydrated when I'm there. It's hot and humid in Naples in the summer time.

As I headed back to my car, I felt an urging to go back and invite the girl to the ladies night that we were having in a couple of weeks. I didn't usually share much of my personal life with the people I deliver to, but I didn't think it would hurt to invite her to the event, so I grabbed a flier and headed back in. I explained the purpose of the night to her, she asked me a few questions, and we ended up chatting for about twenty minutes, with me sharing a bit of my testimony and the relationship that I found with God.

Then she told me that it was really wild that we'd had this conversation because she had a lot of questions about God lately, and she didn't really know where to get answers. I gave her one of my books and invited her to our night out as well as to church and Bible study. I gave her my number and told her to call me anytime.

When I left, she smiled and thanked me for talking with her.

And I got in my car and thanked Jesus for allowing me to be his Sherpa.

―――――――――

Father, thank you for allowing me to be your Sherpa. Thank you for directing my path. And Lord, thank you for giving me that gentle urging when I need to step out for you.

> I Love You Jesus.
> In Your Name I Pray!
> Amen

God's promise for today:

> *"Your attitude should be the same as that of Christ*
> *Jesus: Who, being in very nature God, did not consider*
> *equality with God something to be grasped, but made*
> *himself nothing, taking the very nature of a servant,*
> *being made in human likeness. And being found*
> *in appearance as a man, he humbled himself and*
> *became obedient to death—even death on a cross!"*
> *Philippians 2:5-8*

In Better Hands Now

"My sheep listen to my voice; I know them, and they
follow me. I give them eternal life, and they shall never
perish; no one can snatch them out of my hand."
John 10:27, 28

Natalie Grant has a song called "In Better Hands Now." I was listening to the words the other night, and one line really hit home with me.

She sings, "There is hope when my faith runs out 'cause I'm in better hands now."

That is a powerful line. Now hear me out on this one. You might be thinking, *If she doesn't have any faith left, how can there be hope?*

But the truth is, at some point in our life, in this journey that we are on, we do run out of faith. Or, we may still have a glimmer of faith, but it's fading quickly. Maybe our circumstances are not where we'd like them to be. Or maybe we've been in that place for too long, in our minds, and we begin to lose hope.

We start questioning God. *Are you really who you say you are God? If you are so good, why is this happening to me?* And our faith begins to falter.

But the good news is, the outcome isn't up to us. When I gave my life to God, he took control. Regardless of how strong or weak my faith is, he has dominion.

How many times do we hear, "Pray harder, pray more.

You must not have enough faith" when things go wrong? But the truth is our faith may not have anything to do with our circumstances. We may just be in the middle of a trial. And all the prayers in the world are not going to change the circumstances until it's God's time for it to change.

We don't know his plan for us. But if his plan depends on how much faith we have, well, it could be a rocky roller coaster. On good days, my faith may be strong, on bad days, it may waver. But God's love for us never changes, regardless.

I don't want my hope dependent on me. I am so grateful to know that he's got me covered, regardless of how high the waves seem to be.

———————

Father, thank you for this song that illustrates a principle that is so very vital. Regardless of how much I do or don't do, you are still the same. Father, in this performance based realm that we live in, it is so encouraging to know that you love me, you have my back, and your love doesn't fluctuate with my faith level. You are the constant in this ever changing world.

I Love You Jesus.
In Your Name I Pray,
Amen

God's promise for today:

"For it is by grace you have been saved, through faith—and this not from yourselves, it is the gift of God—not by works, so that no one can boast."
Ephesians 2:8, 9

"You are all sons of God through faith in Christ Jesus."
Galatians 3:26

"Yet to all who received him, to those who believed in his name, he gave the right to become children of God—children born not of natural descent, nor of human decision or a husband's will, but born of God."
John 1:12, 13

"Do not conform any longer to the pattern of this world, but be transformed by the renewing of your mind. Then you will be able to test and approve what God's will is—his good, pleasing and perfect will. "
Romans 12:2

Walking In His Authority

This is another one of those stories that make me say, "Ouch." Ouch, because I messed up in the here and now. Sure, it's somewhat easy to tell you stories of my past, when I didn't know Jesus, when I wasn't walking with him, and I did dumb things and bad things happened to me.

I have an excuse, somewhat, I was in darkness, I didn't know truth. But how do I explain stumbling and falling when I am walking hand in hand with Jesus? That, my friend, is so very hard for me. But, it's life; don't we all mess up when we are trying so hard not to? Even the Apostle Paul had this problem. He tells us:

"I know that nothing good lives in me, that is, in my sinful nature. For I have the desire to do what is good, but I cannot carry it out. For what I do is not the good I want to do; no, the evil I do not want to do—this I keep on doing. Now if I do what I do not want to do, it is no longer I who do it, but it is sin living in me that does it." (Romans 7:18-20)

But James goes on to say, "Therefore confess your sins to each other and pray for each other so that you may be healed. The prayer of a righteous man is powerful and effective." (James 5:16)

I am confessing my stuff to you, and I am praying for you so that I may be healed and it gives you the courage to do the same! That is my objective in sharing, that you understand the lies messing with your emotions, you seek help and you receive healing; that your chains will be broken and your heart set free through Jesus!

I asked God why I had to go through so much pain with this particular issue and he revealed to me that I had to be desperate; I had to really be serious and want it out to receive his healing.

But I am getting ahead of myself here. I haven't told my story yet and I'm already giving you the ending. But truthfully, that is what life with Jesus is like. We know the ending, we know it's good, but we do have to walk through the healing, the journey—our life.

It started out, as it usually does with just a little thing. Those little foxes will get you every time. That is why I am taking the time to share my story with you. So you understand you are not alone in trying to deal with life issues. You are not the only one who lets things get to you. You are not the only one who has struggles. You are not the only one who had a past that messed you up. But, there is hope for you and his name is Jesus!

I let something get under my skin, and as much as I didn't want to admit it or actually let it bother me, it was affecting my joy, my spirit, my peace. I would pray and ask God to take it away, and I'd feel better for a bit, but then the heaviness would set back in, and I couldn't seem to shake it. I started experiencing a sadness that was just overwhelming. It was almost like I was grieving the loss of someone, but no one had died. But that was the intensity of my pain. What it felt like inside – grief.

I sat down one day and focused on my feelings, asking God to show me what was going on inside of me, why I was so sad? Immediately I felt like God was telling me it was a pride issue; a pride issue with me. Ouch…that hurt.

"Pride goes before destruction, a haughty spirit before a fall." (Proverbs 16:18). Can I say ouch again?

First we encounter pride, and then destruction comes into our lives. And I didn't want either.

I prayed and sought God on several occasions about what this whole pride thing was about, and I'd get bits and pieces of revelation, but I never felt like I had true resolution. I live by his peace, and it just wasn't there. Now, please understand, I'm not looking for a happy go lucky sort of life, I know that there are challenges in this world, but if I have God's peace in my heart, the craziness of the world disappears. But there was no peace for me, my heart was heavy, thus I was miserable.

It seemed like the more I prayed, the more stirred up I got. *Ummmm, not working so well*. But I wasn't going to give up. I knew there was some false belief inside of me, messing with my peace, distorting my world, I just didn't know what it was.

During this time, there were a lot of changes going on at my church, and I was trying to attribute my unrest to that. As I've mentioned before, my church family is very important to me, and when things become unsettled, it does affect my spirit.

There seemed to be a feeling of shaking going on, of God's wind blowing through and scattering and pruning off the dead leaves and branches. It was not a comfortable time, and I started believing that I was going to be one of those branches that was going to be blown off. I'm not really sure *why* I thought that, I didn't want to go anywhere, I was content where I was at. I wasn't doing anything I shouldn't be doing; I was walking with God, but again, it goes back to that deception thing. I was being deceived.

As I thought about it more and more, it seemed like what I was grieving was the loss of my church family or the idea that soon I would be shaken off and scattered to the winds. I felt like I was hanging on for dear life, with both hands and both legs, but it wouldn't be enough. It was making me feel sad, and I hated it. But I could not talk myself out of the depression that was setting in. I couldn't hear God's promises for me inside my spirit, and I began feeling weary and worn out.

I didn't feel like God was calling me somewhere else, it wasn't that. It was a more of the feeling that I was going to have to leave, against my will, and it hurt me greatly.

Are you getting the picture? I was basking in a pity party for myself, not enjoying it, not sure why I was in the middle of it, but seemingly not able to escape it either. It really made no sense, but it seemed to be overwhelming me.

One day the emotion became so intense, I couldn't stand it any longer. It's amazing how when you reach the bottom, you realize you have to do something. I'm not sure why it always takes rock bottom for me to *get it*; I guess it goes back to the pride thing. I shouldn't have issues. I shouldn't let life bother me. I should be a *better* Christian. It was all part of the deception I was entangled in.

I was working my courier job that day, and in the afternoon, I wasn't very busy. I decided this was as good a time as any to seek God on this issue, so I pulled up under a tree, put down my car windows, flipped back my car seat and started to pray.

Was I really a branch about to be shaken off? Why was that so intense in my thoughts, in my spirit?

Immediately I sensed God showing me that I was a strong branch, with lots of leaves growing out from me; a covering for those underneath. I wasn't about to be shaken anywhere, I was a firm limb, growing strong from the base.

In John, Jesus tells us:

"I am the vine; you are the branches. If a man remains in me and I in him, he will bear much fruit; apart from me you can do nothing If anyone does not remain in me, he is like a branch that is thrown away and withers; such branches are picked up, thrown into the fire and burned. If you remain in me and my words remain in you, ask whatever you wish, and it will be given you. This is to my Father's glory, that you bear much fruit, showing yourselves to be my disciples."
John 15:5-8

It is to God's glory that we bear fruit—when we bear fruit, we show ourselves to be his disciples! That image brought such peace to my heart, his peace that I'd been seeking the past few weeks, but could not seem to grasp.

As I continued praying, I realized that a big part of my issue was that I was fearful of sharing my true thoughts or feelings with others. I was afraid they'd walk away from me if I didn't always agree with them. This belief stemmed from earlier life experiences where I'd experienced some pretty intense rejection, and it had burned its pain into my mind. I didn't want to go there again, so I would never *rock the boat*, so to speak.

Keep peace at all cost, even my own sanity.

That is never healthy. There is a great book by Henry Townsend and John McCloud called *Boundaries* that explains this concept in depth. I had gone through the study recently, so I knew that my people pleasing tendencies were a heavy burden that I was not meant to bear.

I am not responsible for others' peace, but rather my own. Not that I want to intentionally ever harm another, and I do believe we are to do our best to keep the peace. What I'm talking about is me totally ignoring my true thoughts, or my true self, to not make waves with another. This teaching was fresh in my head; I had just spent eight weeks studying it. I knew what I needed to do, although knowing what to do doesn't always make it *easier* to follow through with correct action.

But God's word tells us, "God is love" and "perfect love drives out fear." (1 John 4:16, 18)

So, if I have God's spirit inside of me, and that spirit is love, then there is no room in me for fear. The fear must leave, and as this becomes revealed knowledge to me, I will pray for God to remove the fear from my spirit and to replace the fear with his love, his perfect love.

In 2 Timothy 1:7 we are told, "For God hath not given us the spirit of fear; but of power and of love, and of a sound mind."

That is what I prayed for as I drove around that afternoon. A spirit of power, of love, and a sound mind. I don't want my mind bouncing around like a ping pong ball. I want my spirit to be calm, regardless of the storms swirling around me.

As I was praying, I started seeing myself as God sees me. I was his child. I was not a pathetic shaking twig, but his daughter, a child of the king. I have all authority given to me by my faith in Jesus. I am the head, not the tail. I am God's chosen vessel. And as I started speaking out, who I am through Christ, my spirit started to swell up, and I saw myself as God sees me.

It was the coolest thing. And as I was sharing my joy with the Lord, I happened to drive by a church and the sign out front proclaimed, "Dark fears flee in the light of God's presence."

Boy could I attest to that! Amen! My fears had fled, and they were definitely replaced with the presence of God's spirit.

I had the sweetest time with God that afternoon. We seemed to be on the same wavelength, finally, and I so enjoyed his presence there with me that day.

Now, before anyone gets the idea that the God of the universe travels around with me in my little Toyota, relax, I'm not psycho, but I have his spirit with me, it goes everywhere that I go and that day, I was so in tune with his spirit in me. It was the most refreshing day!

Now we all know, there is never a testimony, without a test. It's tough to walk through these times of trial, but oh so rewarding to get through to the other side.

And occasionally, God will throw in a little pop quiz, just to make sure we've got this stuff down.

I always hate when that happens, at first. Then I remember his promise: "And God is able to make all grace abound to you, so that in all things at all times, having all that you need, you will abound in every good work." (II Corinthians 9:8)

I remember the truth that he revealed to me, the promise of the future I have with him:

"Do not let your hearts be troubled. Trust in God; trust also in me. In my Father's house are many rooms; if it were not so, I would have told you. I am going there to prepare a place for you. And if I go and prepare a place for you, I will come back and take you to be with me that you also may be where I am." (John 14:1-3)

I spent some time praying, asking God to deal with each and every situation in my life, his way. Not my way, not the way I might have dealt with it in my past, not making the same mistakes again and again, but for God's spirit to guide and direct me in everything I do. Every step I take following him.

No, this isn't about being a goody two shoes, which by the way, I get called quite often. That's a laugh. I've made too many mistakes in my life. I know on my own, I am not good inside, but with God, *all* things become new. Now, each day my focus is to follow God, to walk in the authority that he's given me, as his child. It's not about me, it's all about him!

> We make mistakes, we sin, we fall down, but each time we get up and begin again. We pray again. We seek to follow God again …We confess and begin again … and again … and again
>
> —Richard J. Foster

Working through the Roadblock

"I will break down your stubborn pride and make the sky above you like iron and the ground beneath you like bronze."
Leviticus 26:19

I had a dream one night, while I was going through this season of learning who I was because of who God is. The dream was so realistic to me and the message revealed yet another piece of the puzzle. I love how God gives us answers, sometimes even in our sleep! He doesn't want us struggling through life; he wants us to have victory, in all areas.

In my dream, I was driving along a mountain side, enjoying the scenery, when all of a sudden, I rounded a corner and boom, I stopped dead in my tracks. There was a gigantic roadblock ahead of me.

This wasn't just a stone or two in the road. The entire road was closed. I couldn't move another foot forward. I slammed on my brakes and got out to investigate. There was no way I was getting through; the road was filled with enormous boulders.

As I walked a bit closer, I noticed the fellow on the side of the road with his pick. He asked me if I wanted some help. I thanked him and said yes, I did.

So he swung his tool and slammed into one of the biggest rocks. As he hit the stone, I felt a terrible pain reverberate through my body.

Why is this hurting me, I wondered? The pick hadn't physically touched me, but with each swing, it was as if it was actually penetrating my inner being.

As I stood there, bewildered, taking in the scene, the man turned back around and said, "You're going to have to help me here. There's going to be some work involved in getting this cleared out and it's going to take both of us."

"But why am I feeling the pain?" I asked him.

"Because this is self-will," was his reply, "and it's always the most painful to break through."

But I wasn't sure I could endure the pain?

Then I looked at the man and he said, "It's the only way to go forward, you've got to break through this pile."

So, I picked up the pick and together we started chipping away at those boulders.

God doesn't want us to be prideful and do things our way. Many times, the roadblocks in our lives are just that, our own will getting in the way of God's. And it will stop us in our tracks. But God is so faithful, he doesn't want us to go around the roadblock, he knows we need to work through this challenge to move forward. And he is always there; ready to pick up his ax and help us break through the barrier.

———————————

Father, thank you for standing beside me, for showing me your truth, and for working with me through each and every obstacle.

I Love You Jesus.
In Your Name I Pray,
Amen

God's promise for today:

*"Our steps are made firm by the Lord, when he delights
in our ways; though we stumble, we shall not fall
headlong, for the Lord holds us by the hand."*
Psalm 37:23, 24 (NKJV)

*"Peace I leave with you, my peace I give unto you:
not as the world giveth, give I unto you. Let not
your heart be troubled, neither let it be afraid."*
John 14:27

*"Have mercy on me, O God, according to your unfailing
love; according to your great compassion blot out my
transgressions ... Wash me, and I will be whiter than snow."*
Psalm 51:7

*"I will heal my people and will let them
enjoy abundant peace and security."*
Jeremiah 33:6

What Now?

I not only wanted you to see my struggles and, subsequently, my victories, as those of a *real* person, someone who is just like you, but also to give you a bit of information as to how to apply these concepts to your own life.

If it's just about me, well, it might make an interesting story or not, but I didn't write this to entertain you. I share my life for one reason, to help you understand that you are not alone in this journey. You are not the only one who has felt feelings of inadequacy, of fear, of pain, of loss, of rejection. You are not the only one who has ever been deceived, who has believed the lie.

If God can heal my heart and change my perspective and bring truth to my soul, well, he is more than willing and able to do the same for you. As much as I'd like to be like the Apostle John and believe that I am the disciple that Jesus loved, more than any other, I'm not. Jesus does love me, but he loves you just as much or more, and he is waiting to walk with you through your pain, towards that place of renewal and hope!

I've done a lot of study and research into different types of healing programs, and this book is not a step by step guide. But in a way, everything we do in life is about taking steps; either steps forward or steps backwards.

The first step towards healing is understanding that you have a problem. Or realizing that you have been believing a lie, a wrong perception. Or as it usually happens with me, not really knowing what's wrong, but knowing life isn't right.

That's where you start, by searching your heart and being honest with yourself. Did something stir up inside you while you were reading my story? Did you say, "Wow... that is me!"? Or "I can't believe someone else felt that way."?

You must be willing to want change in your life for God to bring transformation to you. He is all about free will. God will not violate our will, regardless of the consequences. He is a gentleman, always standing by our side, patiently waiting for us to give him the nod, *okay, I can't do this on my own any more, will you help me?*

Or in my situation, as I'm laying bruised and battered at the bottom of the pit. After I've tried and tried and tried again to do it myself and taken yet one more tumble and I cry out in desperation, "Help!"

Either way, he's there.

Maybe someday, and this is my prayer, I will not be so stubborn, I will let him help me sooner rather than later, and I will not have to be battered and bruised before I cry out to him.

I am sharing my story with you because I so want you to understand that I am just like you. It's not easy exposing my soul, baring my past, but because I have been willing, God has healed me! And he's brought me so much peace through the process!

My favorite verse is John 10:10, I've shared it with you before, it is my life mantra, "The thief comes only to steal and kill and destroy; I have come that they may have life, and have it to the full."

The enemy is out to destroy us, but Jesus died, so that we could live! Not a half life, not a defeated, depressed life; but rather a life that is filled to the overflow with his goodness.

Galatians 5: 22, 23 tells us, "But the fruit of the Spirit is love, joy, peace, patience, kindness, goodness, faithfulness, gentleness and self-control." That is what I want my life to be filled with: his good fruit. But to have more of God, I have to have less of myself.

I was thinking about this concept one day and came up with this thought process:

Less of Me ... More of God

If I want to be filled with love, I can't have dislike or scorn for others in my heart.

If I want to be filled with joy, I can't let sadness and sorrow overwhelm my mind.

If I want to be filled with peace, I need to remove worry and fear from my emotions.

If I want to be filled with patience, I have to stop being frustrated and agitated with others.

If I want to be filled with kindness, I cannot be harsh or mean to another.

If I want to be filled with goodness, I cannot harbor evil or wicked thoughts.

If I want to be filled with faithfulness, I cannot be dishonest or disloyal.

If I want to be filled with gentleness, I must remove the roughness in my actions and the hardness in my heart.

If I want to be filled with self-control, I cannot be easily agitated or rash in my actions.

To have more of God will always mean I need less of me. John the Baptist told us: "He must increase, but I must decrease." (John 3:30) It was true for John and it still holds true for us today.

All of these attributes of the Spirit are important to live life, The Jesus Way, but for me, I believe peace is one of the greatest measures of what's going on in our hearts. I know, you've been taught over and over again; *Don't go by your feelings. Live by what you know.*

And that sounds good, on paper, but what if it's not working? What if you *know* in your head God loves you, but you don't *feel* it inside your heart? What if you *know* you are forgiven but you can't *feel* his peace?

I don't want to start some sort of huge theological controversy here, nor am I promoting any new belief system. What I am saying is this, "Until you can get God's love and his truth rooted inside of you, you may not live the life he has for you." And this concept is straight out of his Word: "Therefore confess your sins to each other and pray for each other so that you may be healed. The prayer of a righteous person is powerful and effective." (James 5:16)

There is nothing that compares to the peace of God. I spent over forty years of my life trying to fill that void inside of me with all the wrong things. But once God showed me the lies, ripped them out of me, and filled me up with himself, that was when the peace began to flow through me.

There are three things that I have done consistently over the past few years that I believe have helped me to become the person that God wants me to be. I'm not saying I'm perfect, or even close—my imperfections seem to pop out on a daily basis. But I do know I am not the person I was before I met Jesus and gave my life to him. And I'm not the person

I was five years ago. Through peeling off the layers of lies, I continue to become more like Jesus and less like the old me. I am his new creation.

The three things that I want to encourage you to do to help you stay focused on Jesus are to connect with other believers, stay grounded in God's Word, and spend time in prayer with God each and every day. Not spouting off your to-do list to him, but actually listening to what he is saying to you.

I've always encouraged being part of a church body, not to just *do church*, but to connect with other like-minded people. I became part of a small group study years ago, and it has been my anchor in a sea of challenges and triumphs. Having others to bounce off the good and the bad is imperative to spiritual growth.

"And let us consider how we may spur one another on toward love and good deeds, not giving up meeting together, as some are in the habit of doing, but encouraging one another—and all the more as you see the Day approaching." (Hebrews 10:24, 25)

The other part of my walk that has been so instrumental to my growth is to be in God's Word. If we don't know his instructions for us, how do we expect to walk this journey with him?

I've always been amazed that before I knew Jesus, the Bible was just a book, words on a page that had no meaning or connection to me. But once I turned my life over to him and asked him to guide and direct me, his words have become *life* to me. Words that were written thousands of years ago will now jump out of the page and wrap themselves around my heart.

These words become my guideline for living my life.

They provide answers to those questions that used to swirl around into nothingness. They now give me direction on how to live out this life, God's way.

And we need to spend time alone with God, in prayer. Think about this ... would you consider someone a good friend if you never spent time with them? Of course not. Well, what makes your relationship with God any different? He wants to spend time with you. He wants to heal your heart of all the hurts the world has inflicted upon you. But to do that, you've got to make the effort, you've got to get alone with him, open up and let him do his thing in you. You've got to have communication with him. Not just a Sunday morning church thing, but a 24/7 relationship.

Church is usually two hours on Sunday morning or Saturday night. You have 166 more hours in your week. What you do during those 166 hours is what makes the difference.

Connecting with others while connecting with God is a wonderful start in your journey with Jesus!

This chapter was meant to give you an idea of how to get started with some healing in your life. It's one thing to read a story. It's another to take the principles of that story and use them to make yourself better, inside.

Please don't think this is in any way an all inclusive 'one size fits all' concept. Everyone is different. Everyone has different life experiences. But Jesus knows each of us individually, how we can relate to him. How we hear him. How we receive him. And he will connect with you in a personal way, if you allow him the opportunity to do so.

Spending time with him in prayer, in his Word and with other believers will put you on the path of truth. "You will seek me and find me when you seek me with all your heart." (Jeremiah 29:13)

Life begins each morning...Each morning is the open door to a new world—new vistas, new aims, new tryings.

—Leigh Hodges

God Is Faithful

*"And we know that all things work together
for good to them that love God, to them who
are called according to his purpose."*
Romans 8:28

On March 30, 2008, Bobby lost his job. Not because of any misdeed on his part, but he became an unemployment statistic because of the turn in the economy affecting the construction industry here in Naples.

That day seems like so very long ago, but not because Bobby has been moping about and depressed and time is dragging along, no, quite the opposite. My husband was a little shell shocked that first day, but that is the only day he was really *off*. He has been keeping himself extremely busy since then.

Bobby tore Chase's room apart, painted it and put down new carpet. He cleaned out all the closets and cupboards and then set off doing some things for our friends. He painted one friend's kitchen and den area, spent many days out helping a buddy who puts up pool enclosures, spent a couple of nights helping a friend with a catering business, and then got a job doing some work at another friend's restaurant.

In between, Bobby started his own business, a home watch service. Naples is full of folks who live here half the year, and having someone take care of your home while you're away is becoming a vital service. Bobby is now fully licensed and insured and he has his first two customers.

One month later, he got a new job. Instead of building beautiful homes, he is going to build the swimming pools for them. He is going to be the construction superintendent for a pool company.

It appears the economy hasn't hurt this company, for they are doing well. They offered Bobby a great package to come work for them. He didn't just get *any* job, which honestly, my husband was willing to take. He put his application in anywhere he could think of. But so many places told him he was over-qualified for their company. He really didn't care, he simply wanted to work.

But God gave Bobby a good job, it appears to be as good, or better than the one he left. And in the process, he now has his own business, which he can build up to as large as he wishes.

I am so very proud of Bobby and so very thankful to God. I just knew God had something better for Bobby, and we didn't have to go through a really bad place to get it. Yes, there were a couple of days that I was hoping that God would hurry up and do his thing, but the majority of this month has been a wonderful time of Bobby and I working together, starting something new.

I fell in love with my Bobby while I was working with him, seventeen years ago. I re-fell in love with my husband this past month when I saw the character that he displayed, wanting to take care of his family.

I love bragging on God, on all the cool things that he's done. But honestly, I think this is one of the coolest. I love seeing him take what Satan would use for destruction and turn it into *his glory*!

Thank you Jesus!

———————————

Father, my heart is so full of gratitude today. Not just because you gave Bobby another job, but for allowing me to see the character of the man that I married, in full force during this time that could have been a trial, but was actually such a blessing. Lord, you are truly the best! You are faithful and your word is true—you have worked this all to your good!

> I Love You Jesus.
> In Your Name I Pray,
> Amen

God's promise for today:

> *"I will instruct you and teach you in the way you*
> *hold go; I will guide you with My eye."*
> *Psalm 32:8 (NKJV)*

> *"May the God of hope fill you with all joy and*
> *peace as you trust in him, so that you may overflow*
> *with hope by the power of the Holy Spirit."*
> *Romans 15:13*

> *"The joy of the Lord is your strength."*
> *Nehemiah 8:10*

> *"Peace I leave with you; my peace I give you."*
> *John 14:27*

Epilogue

It's been close to three years since I began this story. I sent it off to the publisher, received back a contract, then it sat on my desk for two years because I didn't have the funds to proceed with publishing.

I mentioned in one of the earlier chapters that we were tight with our funds, and two years later we still are. Bobby has a job, but the economy has hurt the construction industry, and his company is no exception. He earns a weekly paycheck, but there are no benefits, no extras, and that's okay. We are making it. But I promised Bobby that I wouldn't use house money to publish this book because we didn't have it. If God wanted this book published, he would provide the funds. And so I waited. And I waited. And I waited.

Patience is a virtue; but not a trait that comes naturally to me, especially when I am waiting to birth a book. I am fairly impatient by nature, especially when it comes to giving birth. I couldn't wait until the boys were born; I became extremely impatient to meet them. Seeing a book develop from a thought in my head to a book in hand is a similar experience to me, although the boys beat out the books, hands down. But my point is, I've waited patiently for two years for this book to begin the publishing process. And God did provide. Not my timing, but his.

It's been an interesting process, the waiting. A lot has changed in the last two years, but God is still first and foremost. I've started working at my church, my official title is Volunteer Coordinator, but I wear many hats, and I love them all. Every day is Sunday in my world. I no longer spend my days driving around all day, delivering body parts and packages.

There was a time that I felt like God had no more use for me, that all I would ever do was be a delivery girl, a Sherpa. And I had to come to the place inside that if that was my lot in life, that I would embrace it and use every day for God, regardless. It was a hard place to get to. Being a Sherpa really wasn't a place of great esteem, but it was a place of eternal rewards.

One point I want you to understand, as I've read through these stories to edit them, I've realized that the lies are truly gone. "So if the Son sets you free, you will be free indeed" (John 8:36). It's nice to be able to look back over my life and see the difference God has made in me.

Is my life perfect? No, not even close, but truthfully, I don't have as nearly as many struggles as I had even a couple of years ago. I don't let the little foxes get in and spoil my vine. I have learned how to allow God to rule, to put him first and, as a result, my mind is much more stable, clear and not prone to so many roller coaster rides.

If you are already in that place, wonderful, good for you! But for some of you, you may be thinking, *I'm never going to be any better or any different than I am today; I'm always going to be like this.* And that is just not true, if you surrender your life to God and allow him to heal your hurts.

I am a living, walking example of this. You've read my stories, you've seen how messed up I was. As I read these stories I cringe, I was messed up, but today I am not the same person.

If you follow the concepts I shared with you, make a commitment to God, get involved with a group of people who follow Jesus, spend time daily in his word, and work on getting out the lies that mess with your thinking, you will be different too. You will become more and more like Jesus with each passing day, week, month, and year.

I want to encourage you in the words of Winston Churchill, "Never ever ever give up!"

God will never give up on you, as he told Joshua, "No one will be able to stand up against you all the days of your life. As I was with Moses, so I will be with you; I will never leave you nor forsake you" (Joshua 1:5). Please, don't give up on him.

I put together some thoughts for you to ponder a bit before we end this session. I truly do believe that when you immerse yourself in a willingness for truth, truth will come.

May God Richly Bless You!
Joyce

Soul Therapy— What's Going On With Your Heart?

Our souls consist of our minds, our wills, and our emotions, but many times it is simply called our "heart." Our heart dictates the health of our life. We must protect our hearts.

The Bible tells us:

"Above all else, guard your heart, for it is the *wellspring* of life" (Proverbs 4:23).

Many people are lulled into thinking "being a Christian" means they will have no problems, but this is a lie from the enemy.

What is the definition of an enemy?

"One who is out to destroy us."

Jesus, in his prayer to his Father says:

"My prayer is not that you take them out of the world but that you protect them from the evil one" (John 17:15).

We were never meant to have a problem free life but rather the security of knowing who holds our life in his hands.

I. As Christians, We Have An Enemy.

"Be self-controlled and alert. Your enemy the devil prowls

around like a roaring lion looking for someone to devour. Resist him, standing firm in the faith, because you know that your brothers throughout the world are undergoing the same kind of sufferings." (I Peter 5:8, 9)

A. Who do we war against?

"For our struggle is not against flesh and blood, but against the rulers, against the authorities, against the powers of this dark world and against the spiritual forces of evil in the heavenly realms." (Ephesians 6:12)

B. History of Satan's beginning:

"How you have fallen from heaven, O morning star, son of the dawn! You have been cast down to the earth, you who once laid low the nations! You said in your heart, 'I will ascend to heaven; I will raise my throne above the stars of God; I will sit enthroned on the mount of assembly, on the utmost heights of the sacred mountain. I will ascend above the tops of the clouds; I will make myself like the Most High.' But you are brought down to the grave, to the depths of the pit." (Isaiah 14:12-15).

C. His Helpers

"His tail swept a third of the stars out of the sky and flung them to the earth." (Revelation 12:4)

D. Tools of the enemy: Deception—twists the truth—nothing original.

Many deceivers, who do not acknowledge Jesus Christ as coming in the flesh, have gone out into the world. Any such person is the deceiver and the antichrist. (2 John 1:7)

    1. Doubt

        "But when he asks, he must believe and not doubt, because he who doubts is like a wave of the sea, blown and tossed by the wind." (James 1:6)

2. Discouragement

   The Story of Elijah and Jezebel—I Kings 18
3. Distraction

   "But Martha was distracted by all the preparations that had to be made. She came to him and asked, 'Lord, don't you care that my sister has left me to do the work by myself? Tell her to help me!'" (Luke 10:40)

II. As Christians We Have A New Birth—We Need To Have A New Mind.

"Do not conform any longer to the pattern of this world, but be transformed by the renewing of your mind. Then you will be able to test and approve what God's will is—his good, pleasing and perfect will." (Romans 12:2)

A. Who We Are in Christ?

We must understand our position as Christians. We are *no longer sinners*, but rather *saints who sin*. As Christians, we are not *trying to become saints*, but rather *saints who are becoming like Christ.*

"Paul, an apostle of Christ Jesus by the will of God, to the saints in Ephesus, the faithful in Christ Jesus." (Ephesians 1:1)

1. I am secure.

   "Therefore, there is now no condemnation for those who are in Christ Jesus, because through Christ Jesus the law of the Spirit of life set me free from the law of sin and death." (Romans 8:1, 2)
2. I am accepted.

   "Yet to all who received him, to those who believed

in his name, he gave the right to become children of God." (John 1:12)

3. I am significant.

"You are the salt of the earth. But if the salt loses its saltiness, how can it be made salty again? It is no longer good for anything, except to be thrown out and trampled by men. You are the light of the world. A city on a hill cannot be hidden." (Matthew 5:13,14)

B. *Believe* and *receive* who you are, and move forward in your sanctification process or you will be trying to do for yourself, *what God has already done for you.*

C. We can't earn his favor—we already have it. We simply need to *receive* it.

"For it is by grace you have been saved, through faith—and this not from yourselves, it is the gift of God—not by works, so that no one can boast." (Ephesians 2:8, 9)

III. What Hinders Our Growth—Our Walk of Faith?

A. Unforgiveness

"For if you forgive men when they sin against you, your heavenly Father will also forgive you. But if you do not forgive men their sins, your Father will not forgive your sins." (Matthew 6:14, 15)

B. Vows

"Again, you have heard that it was said to the people long ago, 'Do not break your oath, but keep the oaths you have made to the Lord.' But I tell you, Do not swear at all: either by heaven, for it is God's throne; or by the earth, for it is his footstool; or by Jerusalem, for it is the city of the Great King. And do not swear by your head, for you cannot make even one hair white or black. Simply let your 'Yes' be 'Yes,' and your 'No,' 'No'; anything beyond this comes from the evil one." (Matthew 5:33-37)

C. Pride

"God opposes the proud but gives grace to the humble." (James 4:6)

D. Giving in to temptation

"When tempted, no one should say, 'God is tempting me.' For God cannot be tempted by evil, nor does he tempt anyone; but each one is tempted when, by his own evil desire, he is dragged away and enticed." (James 1:13-14)

E. Wrong attitudes and behavior

"The acts of the sinful nature are obvious: sexual immorality, impurity and debauchery; idolatry and witchcraft; hatred, discord, jealousy, fits of rage, selfish ambition, dissensions, factions and envy; drunkenness, orgies, and the like. I warn you, as I did before, that those who live like this will not inherit the kingdom of God." (Galatians 5:19-21)

F. Wrongful speech

"For whosoever would love life and see good days must keep his tongue from evil and his lips from deceitful speech." (I Peter 3:10)

IV. How Do We Find Freedom?

A. Understanding that God is greater than the boogie man.

"'I am the Alpha and the Omega,' says the Lord God, 'who is, and who was, and who is to come, the Almighty.'" (Revelation 1:8)

"You, dear children, are from God and have overcome them, because the one who is in you is greater than the one who is in the world." (I John 4:4)

B. Repent of your sins

    1. Ask God to forgive you for...unforgiveness, pride, bad attitude or wrongful action or making a vow, etc...

    2. Release control of your life back to God.

    Once you have forgiven an individual for each specific offense that you can recall, and then release that person back to the Lord.

> "Those whom I love I rebuke and discipline. So be earnest, and repent." (Revelation 3:19)
>
> "Therefore this is what the LORD says: 'If you repent, I will restore you that you may serve me; if you utter worthy, not worthless, words, you will be my spokesman.'" (Jeremiah 15:19)

    3. Receive God's grace, mercy, and salvation.

> "For God did not appoint us to suffer wrath but to receive salvation through our Lord Jesus Christ." (I Thessalonians 5:9)
>
> "Let us then approach the throne of grace with confidence, so that we may receive mercy and find grace to help us in our time of need." (Hebrews 4:16)
>
> "Blessed is the man who perseveres under trial, because when he has stood the test, he will receive the crown of life that God has promised to those who love him." (James 1:12)

V. Staying in Tune

A. Spend time daily reading God's Word

B. Immerse yourself in praise and worship music

C. Spend time with other believers

D. Spend time with alone with God.

"A lone coal, regardless of how hot it is at any point, will burn itself out if it's left sitting on the side of the hearth alone. We need the support and encouragement of each other to keep our fires burning."

—Joyce Schneider

"And let us consider how we may spur one another on toward love and good deeds. Let us not give up meeting together, as some are in the habit of doing, but let us encourage one another—and all the more as you see the Day approaching."
Hebrews 10:24, 25

And always remember, God has a plan for you.
Keep seeking—He *is* there!

"'For I know the plans I have for you,' declares the LORD, 'plans to prosper you and not to harm you, plans to give you hope and a future. Then you will call upon me and come and pray to me, and I will listen to you. You will seek me and find me when you seek me with all your heart. I will be found by you,' declares the LORD, 'and will bring you back from captivity.'"
Jeremiah 29:11-14

Endnotes

1. ThinkExist.com, Quotes from Billy Graham, last update, Dec. 2010, http://en.thinkexist.com/quotes/billy_graham/4.html

2. Amy Carmichael, A Woman's Prayer for Everyday of the Year, (calendar), March 23, (Bloomington, MN: Garborg's, 2001)

3. ThinkExist.com, Quotes from Billy Graham, last update, Dec. 2010, http://en.thinkexist.com/quotes/Billy_Graham

4. Joanna Weaver, *Having a Mary Heart in a Martha World*, (Colorado Springs, CO.: Waterbrook), pages 17, 18

5. Neil Anderson, *Victory Over the Darkness*, (Ventura, CA.: Regal), page 9

Chili and Chocolate Cake

… MY RECIPE FOR
STAYING ANCHORED
IN THE STORMS OF LIFE

By Joyce Schneider

Chili and Chocolate Cake is not your average inspirational book, and it is as unique as the title. The author shares her message of forgiveness, restoration, and hope for hurting women—especially those who have experienced the loss of a child through abortion, miscarriage, or stillborn birth.

This book is a shining testimony to the power of God to heal the broken heart. Author Joyce Schneider's dramatic life and the miraculous change from a tortured young woman to a great woman of God will encourage every reader. God even used the stability gained from preparing chili and chocolate cake to weave the thread of His grace throughout her troubled life.

Get ready for an outpouring—from the barren days of the past to springs of living waters—rivers that will refresh long after you close the pages of this book.

What others are saying about Joyce Schneider's irst book, *Chili and Chocolate Cake: My Recipe For Staying Anchored In The Storms Of Life*:

"Though not a cookbook, *Chili and Chocolate Cake* does contain the recipe for a life filled with hope, love, and faith in Jesus Christ, regardless of circumstances. Joyce tackles the hard issues in life: our hidden battles with insecurity and insignificance, facing what's phony in us, and coming to the end of desperate attempts to be and do 'enough.' With compassion and warmth, Joyce vulnerably invites readers to become 'real,' to trust Christ beyond what we can see, because only He is 'enough.'"

—Brenda Waggoner , TX, author of
The Velveteen Woman and *Fairy Tale Faith*

"This is a real life book written by a real person who just tells it like it is. She has a way of making you feel like she is sitting beside you telling you her story as you read. Her family is real and the experiences she goes through are things many of us deal with but never had the courage to talk about or share even with a friend. Joyce encourages anyone with past hurts and pains to take a step toward God and allow His healing to occur. I highly recommend *Chili and Chocolate Cake*!"

—Cindy Hollinsgworth, FL

"Joyce Schneider takes you on a journey of her most personal struggles with life and her most profound finding of her spirit. She shares her pain and then rebuilds her life with the acceptance of God and His miracles of truth, love, and the powers to heal. Her honest approach to her life's struggles sparks hope and lights a path to all of us who have experienced life's turmoil. It is a wonderful testimony of finding peace in a world plagued with pain and suffering."

—Erik South, FL

"Joyce Schneider has written this book in a manner that one does not want to put it down until you're finished reading it from cover to cover. She has put her passion, empathy, emotions, and pain in sentences that reach into one's inner self, especially if you have also endured the same type of experience. Through her words, she and her strong faith in God takes the wounded heart out of the darkness and into the light, to be healed with time and trust. I would recommend it to any and every woman, whether they have endured a similar happening in her life or not. There is much to be learned for all."

—B. DeLozier, WA

"Joyce is a 'real' woman who has allowed God to use her to minister to others as she reveals the truth about her past, deals with the heartache of two miscarriages, and finds freedom from guilt and shame. You will be encouraged and challenged through the Scripture and prayers that she weaves through her story in this book."

—Mary Hines, FL

"Joyce Schneider has scored a hit. Tremendous! This book has it all...Life begins and ends with *Chili and Chocolate Cake*...a living classic...a life-changing experience...a spiritual lift!"

—Vicki Gardner, PA

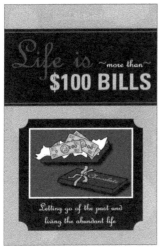

Life is . . . More Than $100 Bills

LETTING GO OF THE
PAST AND LIVING THE
ABUNDANT LIFE

By Joyce Schneider

Popular author Joyce Schneider's newest book, *Life Is More Than $100 Bills*, will hit you where you live. This inspirational book full of life lessons will touch your heart, make you smile, and challenge you to grow in Christ.

It is a motivational book of life lessons geared toward those who want to strengthen their walk of faith. Joyce Schneider offers this personal collection of lessons and true-life stories. In her warm, vulnerable style, this gifted story teller takes the reader along as she faces everyday challenges that test her patience and commitment. Life is more than wasted days, more than empty pursuits, more than misplaced priorities—*Life Is More Than $100 Bills*!

What others are saying about Joyce Schneider's sec-ond book, *LIFE IS More Than $100 Bills!:*

"*Life Is More Than $100 Bills* has the anointing of God on it from the front cover to the last sentence. Joyce tells of the love that only Jesus can give that will change our very nature ... of a faith that surpasses all understanding, a courage that keeps us safe through any kind of ferocious hurricane or storm that blows our way. Yes, 'the things of this world will grow strangely dim, in the light of His glory and grace' rings true through the pages of this unique book."

—Virginia Farless, TN

"Joyce writes about grounding your life in God's econ-omy—the value system based on what the Scriptures reveal as the important things, like trust, obedience, God's grace, and His sovereignty. She gives us an authentic glimpse of what's going on in her heart at times when she's prideful, stubborn, and foolish and shows how God transforms her to become submissive, grateful, and wise, and how God always loves us."

—Brenda Waggoner, TX

"It is such a blessing to read Joyce Schneider's material. It is absolutely as if you are sitting in a room with her and she is sharing the trials of her life's journey along with the triumphs that God has allowed her to obtain. It is amazing and absolutely captivating how you can feel every pain and every victory as she takes you through the trials that she has faced in her life and in her walk with God. And it is wonderful how she translates all of her experiences to where you not only can see them from a worldly view but also from a heavenly perspective. It is apparent that she loves God with all of her heart and she maintains an intimate relationship with Him. The maturity of her spiritual walk is so apparent, but what makes her writings so captivating and receptive is her humility to let others know that she is just like everyone else. Struggling to make it and realizing by God's grace and mercy what He says about every path we find ourselves on in life. Joyce not only shares His Word but she shares the issues in life she has faced and the process she has endured to keep her life on the right path. The same issues that the rest of us encounter each and every day."

—Nancy Dyer, TN

"Joyce Schneider has a singular ability to communicate heart issues in a way that allows the reader to connect with her as an author and at the same time gain insight into God's nature for their own lives. There is nothing more powerful than personal testimonials for reaching beyond the merely theological and gripping the heart and soul with truth, especially when those testimonials reveal the effectual working of God's living Word. Joyce has once again captured the essence of a personal relationship with Christ and related it to us most effectively leaving us with a desire to know Him even more."

—Lawrence Slater, FL

Life is Not About Perfect

A DAILY DOSE OF
ENCOURAGEMENT

By Joyce Schneider

Ever feel like you just aren't getting it? You are not alone. In her third work, *Life Is Not About Perfect,* Joyce Schneider gives us a glimpse into how to enjoy living amidst the trials and tribulations of everyday life. This unique devotional proclaims a message of hope and encouragement through family antics, inspiring us to see life situations for what they truly are–opportunities to live out our faith.

Through the transparency of her own situations, this gifted storyteller gives readers valuable life lessons and leaves them with the revelation that life is about love and living, but... *Life Is Not About Perfect!*

What others are saying about Joyce Schneider's third book, *Life is Not About Perfect:*

"I love Joyce's ability to share everyday life experiences in a way that challenges us with truth from God's Word."
—Mary Hines, Bible teacher,
Pathway Church, Naples, FL

"You will be blessed by Joyce's unusual ability to draw spiritual truth from everyday experiences."
—Kevin Callahan, Pastor of Grace Bible Church,
New Freedom, PA

"You will enjoy each story because it could be your own."
—Cindy Hollingsworth, Bible teacher, Naples, FL

Grass Stains and Giggles

EXPERIENCING GOD IN THE
MIDST OF MOTHERHOOD
By Joyce Schneider

Grass Stains and Giggles by Joyce Schneider invites you to look again in the daily grind of life. Through heartwarming and colloquial tales about her life adventures of parenting, Joyce offers a glimpse of how to live out your faith in real time, every single day. Allow God to nourish your spirit and bring hope through the journey not in spite of, but in the midst of the frenzy of day-to-day affairs. *Grass Stains and Giggles* reminds us that God is ever present in caring for His children if we are willing to listen, even when we don't expect Him to speak.

What others are saying about Joyce Schneider's fourth book, *Grass Stains and Giggles*:

"Joyce's gift for seeing God at work through every detail of her life will encourage the heart, tickle the spirit, and give hope for the journey as she candidly shares the poignant spiritual truths being the mother of two little boys is teaching her."

—Millie Farthing, Director, Celebration of Grace, Women's Retreat Ministry; Regional Speaker Trainer, Stonecroft Ministries

"You have the gift of teaching. I can see it in everything that you write. You so clearly make it easy to understand and applicable by sharing your own personal stories with us and how it ties into what you are sharing in regards to the Word. You make it real."

—Kristi Cole, Texas

"You have a God-given gift to 'meet me right where I am.' I enjoy your stories and your simplistic message. Your ability to open my eyes to things that are right in front of me can only come from one place!"

—Brenda Morris, Naples, FL

"Joyce has been blessed with the ability to share God's miraculous touch on our everyday lives. Joyce brings the joys of motherhood to a heavenly level that brings joy and laughter to your soul. Thank you Joyce for your obedience to Gods call on your life! We have been blessed by your work!"

—Renee Relf, Author *Evil In Paradise, The Triumph of Faith and Love over Greed and Power.*